The Military History of World War II
Volume 3

LAND BATTLES: NORTH AFRICA, SICILY, AND ITALY

The Military History of World War II: Volume 3

LAND BATTLES: NORTH AFRICA, SICILY, AND ITALY

by Trevor Nevitt Dupuy
COL., U.S. ARMY, RET.

FRANKLIN WATTS, INC.
575 Lexington Avenue • New York 22

To Rosie

Library of Congress Catalog Card Number: 62-11175
Copyright © 1962 by Franklin Watts, Inc.
Printed in the United States of America

3   4   5   6   7

PHOTO CREDITS

*Pages 2, 24, 28, 31, 43, 60, 61, 63, 67, 69, 70, 74, 75, 76,
77, 79, 81, 84, 86, 87* — PHOTOS FROM WIDE WORLD.
*Pages 5, 8, 9, 12, 16, 19, 20, 32, 35, 37, 39, 46, 50, 51,
53, 56, 57, 63* —OFFICIAL U.S. ARMY PHOTOGRAPHS.

Maps by Dyno Lowenstein.

Contents

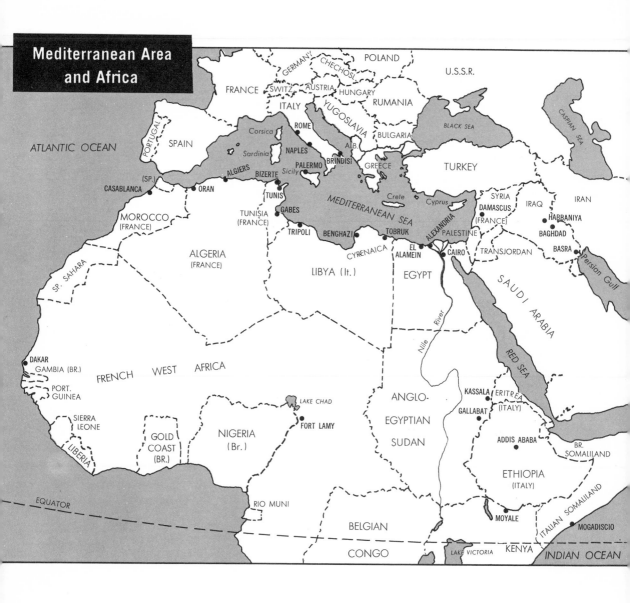

Mediterranean Area and Africa

POLAND

GERMANY   CHECHOSL.

FRANCE   SWITZ.   AUSTRIA   HUNGARY   U.S.S.R.

ITALY   YUGOSLAVIA   RUMANIA

ATLANTIC OCEAN   PORTUGAL   SPAIN   Corsica   ROME   BULGARIA   BLACK SEA

Sardinia   NAPLES   ALB.   CASPIAN SEA

ALGIERS   BIZERTE   PALERMO   BRINDISI   GREECE   TURKEY

CASABLANCA   (SP.)   ORAN   Sicily   Crete   Cyprus   SYRIA   IRAQ   IRAN

TUNIS   MEDITERRANEAN SEA   DAMASCUS   (FRANCE)

MOROCCO   TUNISIA   GABES   (FRANCE)   HABBANIYA

(FRANCE)   (FRANCE)   TRIPOLI   BENGHAZI   TOBRUK   ALEXANDRIA   BAGHDAD

ALGERIA   CYRENAICA   EL   PALESTINE   BASRA

(FRANCE)   LIBYA (It.)   ALAMEIN   CAIRO   TRANSJORDAN   Persian Gulf

SP. SAHARA   EGYPT   SAUDI ARABIA

RED SEA

DAKAR   Nile River

GAMBIA (BR.)   FRENCH   WEST   AFRICA   KASSALA   ERITREA

PORT.   ANGLO-   GALLABAT   (ITALY)

GUINEA   LAKE CHAD   EGYPTIAN

SIERRA   FORT LAMY   SUDAN   ADDIS ABABA   BR.

LEONE   SOMALILAND

LIBERIA   GOLD   NIGERIA   ETHIOPIA

COAST   (Br.)   (ITALY)

(BR.)   ITALIAN SOMALILAND

EQUATOR   RIO MUNI   MOYALE   MOGADISCIO

BELGIAN   LAKE VICTORIA   KENYA   INDIAN OCEAN

CONGO

World War II Reaches the Mediterranean

Italy Declares War

ON JUNE 10, 1940, Premier Benito Mussolini, dictator of Fascist Italy, declared war on France and Great Britain. This was a safe time for the Italians to make such a declaration because French and British armies had just been defeated by the new German *blitzkrieg* (lightning war) in the Battle of Flanders. German *panzer* (tank) divisions were at that very moment slashing the remnants of the French army to bits in the Battle of France.

Mussolini did not think that Italy would have to do much fighting. He was sure that France and Britain would soon surrender. When that happened, he expected to share the spoils of victory with Adolf Hitler, Nazi dictator of Germany. What Mussolini particularly wanted was to occupy some French and British colonies in Africa and to seize control of the Suez Canal from the British.

Mussolini guessed right about France. On June 25 the French surrendered to the Germans, and the government of France, at Vichy, came under the control of Hitler.

But the Italian dictator was wrong in expecting Britain to surrender. The English people had just chosen Winston Churchill as their prime minister, and they rallied behind his promise to lead their fight for as long as it might take to destroy Hitler's Nazism and Mussolini's Fascism.

So, to his surprise, Mussolini found that he would have to fight a war with Britain in order to expand in Africa and to gain control of the Mediterranean Sea and the Suez Canal. He was still confident

1

With a list to port, and ablaze from bow to stern, this Axis cargo vessel, hit by R.A.F. planes, is headed for the bottom of the Mediterranean.

that the fight would be an easy one, however, because when the defeated British had been carried from Dunkirk back to England after the Battle of Flanders, they had been forced to abandon all their heavy equipment: guns, tanks, trucks, and the like.

Mussolini was sure that every available British soldier, every new tank and gun produced in British factories, most of the ships of the Royal Navy, and most of the aircraft of the Royal Air Force would be needed in England to meet the threatened German invasion of Britain. And so it was that, during the summer of 1940, the Italians slowly got ready to march into British possessions in Africa.

Britain's "Lifeline"

CHURCHILL and the British military leaders knew perfectly well what Mussolini was planning. Although they were desperately short of trained soldiers and equipment, they were determined that they would not let the Italians win in the Mediterranean and in Africa without a real fight.

England, a small but densely populated island, had to import not only food and the other necessities of life, but also the raw materials necessary for war production. Many of these things came by ship from Britain's great empire in Asia and the Pacific. Practically all of Britain's commerce to and from that part of the world followed the sea route that passed through the Mediterranean Sea, the Suez Canal, and the Red Sea. This sea route had long been known as "the lifeline of the British Empire."

This was also the route that would bring reinforcements to the British army from India, Australia and New Zealand. If the "lifeline" was cut, then England would be in serious danger. The alternate route around Africa, by way of the Cape of Good Hope, was about twice as long as the one through the Suez Canal. Merchant ships using this alternate route would take much longer to make the trip, and this would dangerously delay the arrival of food and other materials England needed to stay alive and fighting.

The easiest place for the Italians to cut the British lifeline was in the Middle East. That was the area where the sea route was closely bordered by the lands of the Red Sea and the eastern Mediterranean. Italy had several colonies in this region, and it was here that Mussolini was building up military strength. Churchill's government realized that they must strengthen nearby British possessions in order to keep the Italians from gaining control of this important area.

Even while the German armies were assembling in northern France, Belgium, and Holland in preparation for an invasion of England, and while the German *Lufftwaffe* — Hitler's air force — had begun the air Battle of Britain, Churchill and his military advisers agreed that they must scrape up reinforcements to be sent to

3

the Middle East. In August, 1940, Britain's only armored brigade was sent to Egypt. This would soon be followed by an entire newly built armored division.

British Setbacks in Africa

BRITAIN's buildup of its armored forces in the Middle East came none too soon. The Italians had already begun to move to gobble up the British possessions along the Mediterranean and Red seas. In August, 1940, Italian troops from Ethiopia invaded British Somaliland and quickly overran the very small garrison of that colony. At the same time, other Italian troops began to move westward from Ethiopia into the Sudan in order to seize the upper Nile Valley. They quickly captured Kassala and Gallabat, while more Italian troops moved south to capture Moyale, in the northern part of the British colony of Kenya. Meanwhile, a powerful Italian army was preparing to march from Libya across northern Egypt to seize the Suez Canal.

Once more the Italians were surprised. The stubborn British neither ran away nor surrendered. Hastily the Italians changed their plans. They would postpone their offensives from Ethiopia until they had captured the Suez Canal. Then they could use the canal to send more troops by sea to Ethiopia, and from there overland into the Sudan and Kenya.

The Italian invasion of Egypt, which started the advance from Libya toward the Suez Canal, began on September 13, 1940. It was under the command of Field Marshal Rodolpho Graziani, whose army was about 200,000 strong and supported by a powerful air force. Graziani reached Sidi Barrani, in northwestern Egypt, then stopped. He was worried about the difficulties of supplying his army over the forbidding, rocky Western Desert that stretched out over northern

4

An Italian field kitchen in Tunisia. Motorcycle carts wait to carry food to troops engaged in action.

Egypt and northeastern Libya, so he gathered a great store of supplies near Sidi Barrani and constructed a pipeline to bring water to his frontline troops. At the same time he built a series of fortifications stretching inland for about 40 miles from the seacoast.

It was at about this time that the British suffered a setback in western Africa. There the Vichy French defenders of Dakar repulsed an effort by the British to land a force of General de Gaulle's Free French troops to gain control of French West Africa.

Thus, as 1940 approached its close, Germany's grip on the French colonies of northern and western Africa was tightening through its control of the puppet French government in Vichy. At the same time the Italian buildup behind Sidi Barrani had become so formidable that it seemed that the scanty British forces in Egypt could not possibly stop Italy from seizing the Suez Canal.

But General Sir Archibald Wavell, in command of British Middle East forces, had not given up hope.

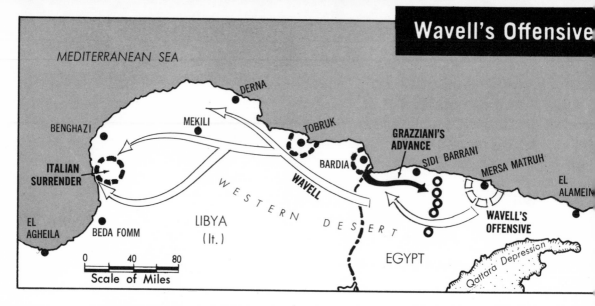

Wavell's Offensives

Wavell's Problems

GENERAL WAVELL was responsible for all British military interests in the Middle East. With forces totaling less than 100,000, he had to face the threat of almost half a million Italian soldiers in Ethiopia and Libya.

In addition, the French garrison of Syria — controlled by the pro-German Vichy government in France — threatened British forces in Palestine. At the same time German agitators were secretly undermining British influence in Iraq, the country that was the main source of British oil and gasoline supplies. Finally, Italy had begun an invasion of Britain's ally, Greece. Wavell had been ordered to send to Greece much of his small air force and large quantities of scarce supplies and equipment. With this assistance, the sturdy Greek soldiers had been able to repulse the Italian invasion, and so Wavell did not have to send them any ground soldiers.

6

Few military leaders in modern history have had to face such widespread, overwhelming threats. But Wavell was not an ordinary man. A gifted writer and an amateur poet, he was at the same time a strong-willed, imaginative, skillful professional soldier.

Wavell had to keep some troops in the Sudan and in Kenya to check the Italians in Ethiopia. He also had small forces in Palestine and in Iraq to keep an eye on German and Vichy-French activities in the Middle East. But he concentrated every other available man and gun in western Egypt to oppose Graziani's army, since this was the main threat to the Suez Canal and to Britain's lifeline.

First British Offensive in the Western Desert

THE BROAD, desolate region stretching for hundreds of miles on both sides of the border between Egypt and Libya is known as the Western Desert. Wavell's small army in this area was called the Western Desert Force. It was concentrated opposite the Italian fortifications near Sidi Barrani, under the immediate command of Lieutenant General Richard N. O'Connor.

O'Connor was a vigorous, forceful soldier. Under Wavell's supervision he prepared the Western Desert Force for an attack against the Italians. By early December, 1940, the force had grown to three divisions, and totaled about 40,000 men. This was less than one-quarter the size of Graziani's Tenth Italian Army.

Despite the superior Italian strength, Wavell ordered the attack to start on December 9. O'Connor quickly found a gap in the Italian defenses. The British dashed through this gap, completely surprising Graziani. The main British force raced for the coast at Sidi Barrani, while detachments slashed at the rear of the confused Italian units. Within two days nearly 40,000 Italians surrendered, while the rest

7

Italian prisoners file to trucks that will carry them to Allied prisoner-of-war camps.

streamed westward toward Libya, completely demoralized.

Wavell ordered an immediate pursuit. Less than a week from the initial British attack all of the Italians had been driven from Egypt. With scarcely a pause, the British continued their drive into Libya. This was "lightning war" as vigorous as any the Germans had waged in Europe.

While part of the British Western Desert Force chased the Italians westward along the single seacoast road, British tank units rushed inland by a more direct route, across the flat, rocky desert, in order to get behind the retreating foe. Bardia, Tobruk, and Derna were captured by the racing British columns. More and more Italian prisoners were taken. Making another bold dash across the bulge of Cyrenaica, the British tanks cut off and captured the last remaining organized segment of Graziani's army south of Benghazi on February 7, 1941.

In two months the Western Desert Force had destroyed the effectiveness of the Italian Tenth Army. They had killed or wounded more than 10,000 Italians, and had captured over 130,000 men as well as vast quantities of guns, tanks, and supplies. Their own losses were less than 2,000 men killed or wounded.

Wavell had hoped to be able to continue his advance to Tripoli, and to drive the remaining Italians completely from North Africa. But now the British government had another problem to solve — the situation in Greece. The Greeks had repulsed the Italian invasion of their country, but there were growing indications that Hitler would send German troops to help Mussolini overrun Greece. Churchill, feeling that Britain was honor-bound to give her Greek ally all possible assistance, ordered Wavell to stop his advance in Libya and to send all available troops to Greece at once.

Wavell knew that he could not send enough men to stop a full-scale German invasion of Greece. But he also realized that he must try to do everything he could to help the gallant Greek people in the de-

A "sapper" from the British Eighth Army uses a detector to remove mines from the road near Tripoli.

fense of their independence. And he knew that, as a soldier, he must obey the orders of his government. So he rushed most of the veterans of the Western Desert Force across the Mediterranean to Greece, leaving only one infantry division and one untrained armored brigade at El Agheila to defend his conquest of Cyrenaica.

British Offensives in East Africa

MEANWHILE, the tiny British garrisons of the Sudan and of northern Kenya had been able to prevent any further Italian advances from Ethiopia or Somaliland. As soon as he had won his first smashing victories over the Italians on the Mediterranean coast, Wavell resolved to try to win the same kind of successes in East Africa. He put the British forces in Kenya and the Sudan under the command of Lieutenant General Sir Alan Cunningham and sent him reinforcements from the victorious Western Desert Force, as well as some new arrivals from Britain, South Africa, and India. Then, even though Cunningham's army of about 70,000 men was less than one-third the strength of Italian forces in East Africa, Wavell ordered an attack.

The British drive into Ethiopia and Italian Somaliland began on January 15, 1941. The Italians, demoralized by Wavell's successes in Libya, fell back after offering slight resistance. Cunningham and his main forces pressed into the mountainous interior of Ethiopia. Columns from Kenya continued to drive northward into Italian Somaliland. Others from the northern Sudan advanced into Eritrea.

On February 26, the British entered Mogadiscio, capital of Italian Somaliland. Addis Ababa, capital of Ethiopia, was captured on April 6. In May the main Italian army surrendered, ending all organized resistance in East Africa. By the end of the year all outlying regions of Italian East Africa were firmly occupied by the British.

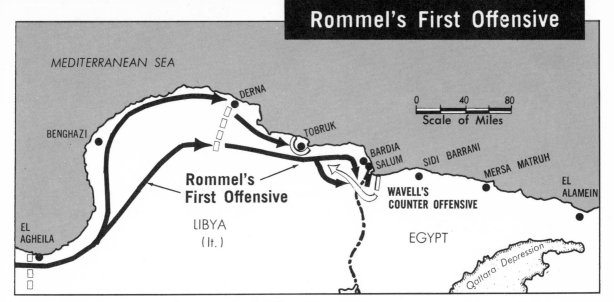

MEDITERRANEAN SEA

DERNA

BENGHAZI

TOBRUK

BARDIA
SALUM

SIDI BARRANI

MERSA MATRUH

EL
ALAMEIN

0   40   80
Scale of Miles

**Rommel's
First Offensive**

**WAVELL'S
COUNTER OFFENSIVE**

EL
AGHEILA

LIBYA
(It.)

EGYPT

Qattara Depression

Crises in the Middle East

Arrival of Rommel and the Afrika Korps

ALTHOUGH the British government had been suspicious that Hitler was planning to help his Italian allies conquer Greece, it did not suspect that he had also decided to send German troops to Libya to bolster the crumbling Italian African empire. Hitler recognized the importance of the British lifeline through the Mediterranean Sea and the Suez Canal, and he was determined to cut that line by sea and air attacks from bases in North Africa, Sicily, Italy and Greece. Also, he was preparing to fight Russia, and he believed that he could defeat the Soviets more easily if he could attack through the Caucasus from the Middle East as well as from eastern Europe.

In March, 1941, therefore, at the same time the German forces were preparing to invade the Balkans and to conquer Greece, Hitler sent two divisions to Tripoli, the capital of Libya. Both of these — one armored and the other an infantry division — were specially

11

equipped and trained for fast-moving desert warfare. To command this newly created *Afrika Korps* and the Italian forces in Libya, Hitler selected General Erwin Rommel, who had distinguished himself in command of a *panzer* division in the German *blitzkriegs* in Flanders and France in May and June, 1940.

And so, while most of Wavell's Western Desert Force was being ferried across the Mediterranean to Greece, Rommel began grouping his own divisions and the remnants of Graziani's army in preparation for another attack toward the Suez Canal.

Rommel's First Offensive

ON MARCH 24, Rommel made a sharp raid against the small British force holding advanced positions at El Agheila. Immediately discovering how weak the British were, he continued his attack into Cyrenaica. By April 3 he had captured Benghazi, and continued to drive the British back along the seacoast road. Just as Wavell and O'Connor had done in January, he sent a powerful tank column roaring inland across the desert bulge of Cyrenaica toward Tobruk to cut off the British retreat. On April 6, the British suffered the

General Erwin Rommel.

greatest loss of the campaign: one of Rommel's *panzer* columns captured Wavell's sturdy, able assistant, General O'Connor, while he was on reconnaissance in the desert.

Gathering together the few remaining British units in Egypt, Wavell rushed them to Tobruk, and there the troops retreating from El Agheila were ordered to stop and fight. Rommel's tank column swept up against the hasty British defenses on April 10, and he immediately attacked. For five days a bitter battle raged outside Tobruk, but despite the ferocity of German attacks, the British defenders stood firm. And as more German and Italian troops reached the outskirts of the city, Wavell rushed supplies and equipment by sea to the defenders. When the battle was over, the British had lost all of their conquests in Libya except Tobruk.

Rommel sent a column to seize Bardia and Salum, just inside the Egyptian border, but he could make no further advance into Egypt toward the Suez Canal so long as the British threatened his line of communications by continuing to hold Tobruk. He made another violent assault on the besieged city at the end of April, but again the British defenders repulsed the attacks.

Meanwhile Wavell had collected a few more units from Palestine and East Africa, plus a few reinforcements from England and India, and had built up a new line of defense just inside the Egyptian border, east of Salum.

Catastrophe in Greece and Crete

AT THE SAME TIME that Rommel was driving the British from Cyrenaica, the main fighting force of Wavell's armies was fighting desperately in Greece. The German drive into Yugoslavia and Greece had begun on April 6. Though greatly outnumbered, the British, under the command of General Maitland Wilson, fought bravely and successfully. But the combined strength of the Italian and German offensive was too much for the heroic little Greek army. As the Greeks fell back, the British were also forced to withdraw, first to central Greece, then further south. Finally, when they could resist no more, the Greeks surrendered. On April 27, under overwhelming German aerial attack, the British began to evacuate their troops from Greece. British losses, both army and navy, were very great.

Some of the British troops were withdrawn to Egypt, where Wavell threw them into the line near Salum. Most of the remainder were sent to Crete, to try to prevent the Germans from seizing that island.

As the British had expected, the Germans made a powerful airborne attack on Crete on May 20, and followed it with more. Although the British army and navy fought vigorously, they were terribly short of supplies. By the end of May, the Germans had succeeded in driving the British from Crete and capturing many of the defending troops.

Iraq and Syria

As IF these terrible defeats in Libya, Greece, and Crete were not enough, Wavell was faced by other serious threats. Hoping to be able to drive the British completely from the Middle East, Hitler had begun to stir up trouble in both Syria and Iraq.

Syria had been under French rule since World War I, and it had remained under the control of the German-controlled Vichy government after the fall of France in June, 1940. For a year the British in the Middle East had been keeping a watchful eye on Syria's 35,000 pro-German French troops.

Iraq had been a British possession, but had been granted independence in 1932. At that time the newly independent government of Iraq had signed a treaty of alliance with Britain, agreeing that the British should keep military bases at Basra and Habbaniya to help protect Iraq's very valuable oil wells. These wells provided practically all of the oil and gasoline used by British forces in the Middle East and in India.

During the early days of the war a pro-Nazi Arab politician named Rashid Ali had become Prime Minister of Iraq. In late April of 1941, as Rommel was driving the British back in Libya and other German troops were overrunning Greece, Rashid Ali decided that the British were about to lose the war. He did not need much encouragement from Hitler to stir up his people against the British garrisons at Basra and Habbaniya.

On May 2, Iraqi troops surrounded and attacked the base at Habbaniya. The British government immediately sent troops by sea and air from India to Basra. And Wavell — even though his troops were fighting desperately near Tobruk and in East Africa, and were preparing for the German attack on Crete — scraped together a few reserves in Palestine and sent them across the desert to the relief of the hard-pressed defenders of Habbaniya.

Meanwhile, Hitler had begun to send German military advisers by air from Greece to Bagdad, capital of Iraq. Soon German transport planes were bringing in quantities of military supplies, and these were followed by German and Italian fighter planes, which began to establish an operational base at Mosul.

By that time the British had gathered enough forces for Wavell to order an attack. Royal Air Force planes struck the new German and Italian air base at Mosul. The troops from Palestine reached Habbaniya, then combined with the garrison there to advance on

German anti-tank trap in Libya.

Bagdad. Rashid Ali fled from the country. British troops entered Bagdad on May 30, and on May 31, peace was established.

While all of this had been going on in Iraq, numbers of German officers and politicians had begun to arrive in Syria, where they were increasing their control of the French troops and threatening the British forces in Palestine and Iraq. Churchill ordered Wavell to drive the Germans out of Syria. So, even though his troops were fighting desperately in the Western Desert, in Crete and in Iraq, Wavell gathered together 20,000 men for an invasion of Syria.

On June 8, 1941, the small British force attacked northward from Palestine. After a short advance toward Damascus, the British were stopped by superior numbers of French. Wavell then ordered his troops in Iraq to move into the fight. Damascus was captured by the British on June 21, and the French commander, General Dentz, finally surrendered on July 12.

By his victories in Iraq and Syria, Wavell had rid himself of the

16

dangerous threats to the rear of the British position in the Middle East, but his overall situation was still desperate. About 30,000 of the very best troops in his army had been lost in the battles in Greece and in Crete. His forces in the Western Desert had been badly beaten by Rommel, whose advance into Egypt was held up only by the small British force blockaded in Tobruk. German and Italian reinforcements and supplies were pouring into Libya to build up Rommel's army. German airplanes in Greece and Crete were bombing British bases in the Suez Canal area, and had driven the British Navy from the eastern Mediterranean.

The British Strike Back in the Western Desert

Wavell's Counteroffensive

FOLLOWING the defeats in Greece and Libya, the British government rushed reinforcements to hard-pressed General Wavell. At the same time, Churchill sent the general frequent messages asking him to counterattack the Germans in the Western Desert and to rescue the British garrison in the besieged fortress of Tobruk.

Wavell was able to send some reinforcements and supplies to Tobruk by sea, but he knew that Rommel was preparing to renew his attacks on the fortress. Wavell hoped that the troops in Tobruk could hurl back any further German and Italian attacks, but he could not be sure. So, under the pressure of the messages from Churchill, Wavell hastily prepared for another offensive in the Western Desert, even though British troops were still fighting in Crete, Iraq, and

Syria. He managed to assemble only two divisions to attack the large concentration of Germans and Italians in their positions at Salum and Bardia on the Egyptian-Libyan frontier, but he remembered that two divisions had been enough to smash Graziani's army in the same area six months earlier. He expected that the troops in Tobruk could break out to strike the rear of Rommel's army at the same time as the main attack got started.

The counteroffensive began on June 15. Almost immediately Wavell and his troops realized that things had changed in the six months since their initial great victory over the Italians. In the first place, Rommel was no Graziani. Under his inspiring leadership, not only did his German troops fight back with their usual ferocity, but the Italian troops, too, fought bravely. And this time Wavell did not have a desert tank-fighter like O'Connor to lead his attacking troops. The British soldiers, most of them recently arrived reinforcements, were neither so well trained nor so confident as the troops he and O'Connor had led in the battles half a year earlier; most of these veterans had been lost in Greece and Crete.

Another thing that was different was the way in which Rommel and his *Afrika Korps* used a light but powerful German all-purpose artillery gun. This gun was called the "Eighty-eight" because its muzzle was 88 millimeters — about 3½ inches — in diameter. This cannon was small enough to be towed easily across the desert by a light truck. Its thirty-pound projectiles, hurled with great power, speed, and accuracy, were effective against airplanes, against infantry, and were particularly effective against tanks. The German tankers were very clever in pretending to run away, and thus tricking British tanks into chasing after them. The fleeing German tanks would then lead the unsuspecting British into an ambush where a deadly Eighty-eight would be hidden behind a rocky ledge, or in a dry stream bed.

18

Rommel threw back the attacks of the Tobruk garrison. His line of fortifications held firm against the British attacks along the rugged Egyptian-Libyan border. And as British tanks swept around his south flank, across the open desert, Rommel sent a tank column even further south. It hit the British tanks in the flank and rear, and captured numbers of the supporting trucks that were carrying food, gasoline, and ammunition. After three days of furious fighting, Wavell was forced to acknowledge defeat, and to withdraw the remnants of his attacking forces into Egypt.

Clouds of dust and difficult terrain mark the way as the British Eighth Army pushes across the Libyan desert in North Africa.

New British Commander in the Middle East

CHURCHILL had been a great admirer of Wavell, and he probably realized that he had forced his fine general to attack before he was ready. But the British Prime Minister now thought that Wavell had become exhausted by his intensive efforts, and discouraged by his succession of defeats, even though these were beyond his control. Reluctantly Churchill relieved Wavell of his command in the Middle East, and sent him to command India.

Fortunately Churchill had another capable general to send in Wavell's place — General Sir Claude Auchinleck, who had been commanding British forces in India. Auchinleck arrived in the Mid-

An American-made Sherman tank is returned to the British Eighth Army after repairs.

dle East early in July, 1941, and immediately began to prepare for another offensive against Rommel.

Reinforcements of troops from Britain and India continued to arrive in Egypt. At the same time, the first American "Lend-Lease" equipment began to reach Egypt, and this included large numbers of American light tanks to replace those Rommel had destroyed or captured in April and June. Auchinleck reorganized the Western Desert Force into the Eighth Army and worked unceasingly to prepare it for a new offensive. As direct commander of the Eighth Army, he appointed General Alan Cunningham, who had just completed the reconquest of East Africa from the Italians. By the middle of November the British army had attained a strength of seven divisions and about 700 tanks.

All in all, the British were now much better prepared in the Middle East than they had been at any time during the war. Tobruk had been reinforced again. British air and naval units had recovered their control of much of the eastern Mediterranean Sea. This time these units were able to concentrate against the enemy in Libya instead of having to scatter their efforts all over the Middle East.

But that enemy in Libya was a very formidable one. Although most German supplies and reinforcements were being used up in the great battles then going on in Russia, making it impossible for Rommel to build up his army as rapidly as the British, the German general still had three German divisions in his *Afrika Korps*, plus six Italian divisions. And although Hitler had ignored most of Rommel's pleas for more men and supplies, the German general's army was about the same overall size as Auchinleck's. Rommel had only about two-thirds as many tanks as Auchinleck, but most of these were more powerful than the British tanks. And he still had plenty of the deadly Eighty-eights.

21

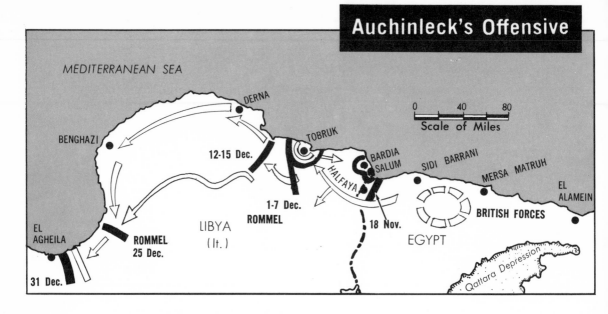

Map labels: MEDITERRANEAN SEA · DERNA · BENGHAZI · TOBRUK · 12-15 Dec. · BARDIA SALUM · SIDI BARRANI · MERSA MATRUH · EL ALAMEIN · HALFAYA · 1-7 Dec. ROMMEL · 18 Nov. · BRITISH FORCES · LIBYA (It.) · EL AGHEILA · ROMMEL 25 Dec. · EGYPT · Qattara Depression · 31 Dec. · 0 40 80 Scale of Miles

Auchinleck's Offensive

THE BRITISH now had a three-to-one superiority in the air. Rommel's long-range reconnaissance planes were quickly chased away by British Hurricane and Spitfire fighters. Because of this, the German commander had not been able to learn exactly where the British troops were. He was completely surprised when Auchinleck launched a powerful offensive on November 18, 1941.

During the next two weeks one of the most confused, hard-fought, seesaw battles of history took place across the vast, desolate Western Desert south of Tobruk and Salum. Once more the British tanks dashed around the right flank of the Axis fortifications below Bardia, Salum and Halfaya Pass. At the same time the British troops in Tobruk attacked to break out of the surrounding ring of German and Italian entrenchments. Despite fierce resistance, the British forged ahead. On November 21, the Tobruk garrison broke through the siege lines.

But violent though the British attack had been, Rommel's response was just as violent. The defenders of Tobruk were thrown back with heavy losses, and the siege lines were re-established. And while the Eighty-eights took a terrible toll of the British tanks, Rommel and his *panzers* struck back. The whole British advance was stopped. It looked like another British defeat.

On November 23, General Cunningham started to withdraw, but Auchinleck flew to the front lines and ordered the retreat to stop. Sending for reinforcements and supplies, he took personal command of the Eighth Army, and even while fierce fighting continued, he got ready to renew the attack.

Now Rommel himself decided to attack. Leading two German *panzer* divisions, he cut through the British left flank units and raided deep behind their lines, back into Egypt. Although the British were surprised by this daring stroke, they clung grimly to the positions they had won. Rommel captured a number of rear-area British troops and supplies, but he in turn was surprised when he realized that his bold raid had not frightened Auchinleck or the Eighth Army into a retreat.

In a war made more bitter than most by the frightfulness of Adolf Hitler, the British had good reason to hate all Germans. But, almost against their will, they found themselves admiring and respecting an enemy who was both a hard-fighting soldier and a courteous gentleman. During his raid behind the British lines Rommel captured a field hospital, full of wounded men. Allowing British doctors to continue their work of saving lives, Rommel took time to leave his tank and walk through the hospital's tents, passing words of encouragement to the patients through an interpreter. It is little wonder that the British soldiers admired and respected him almost as much as they did their own leaders.

Rommel had barely fought his way back to his own main army

Long streamers of exploding munitions on an Allied cargo ship hit by German dive bombers streak across the sky from a mushroom of smoke and fire.

when, on November 26, Auchinleck renewed his attack. While part of the British army struck along the coastal road toward Tobruk, British armored columns again swung south through the desert to get behind Rommel's front lines. On November 27 the defenders of Tobruk broke out again to join with the British troops near the coast. Rommel counterattacked fiercely. Once more he drove the defenders back into the fortress, and smashed back the main British attack. He then tried to advance to relieve the German and Italian troops cut off in the fortifications of Bardia and Salum, but this time he was thrown back with heavy losses.

Stubbornly Auchinleck and his British troops returned to the attack. Once more they linked up with the Tobruk garrison — and this time the link held. As British tanks continued to advance south of Tobruk, Rommel realized that he had been beaten. On December 7, he began a skillful, hard-fighting withdrawal to a line just west of Tobruk.

But Auchinleck again sent his tanks out into the desert to get around and behind the Axis entrenchments. Rommel, short of supplies, his line of retreat threatened by the British advance, realized that he must withdraw further, or his whole army would be cut off. On December 15 he began to pull back rapidly past Benghazi. On December 31 he stopped and established a new entrenched defensive position at El Agheila. He was back almost to the point where he had started his first offensive at the beginning of April.

Auchinleck followed closely. The British tanks sweeping around the great bend of the coastal road past Benghazi reminded the men of a horse race on an English racetrack. They began to call those wild tank races across the desert the "Benghazi Handicaps." This offensive, they said, was the third running of the Benghazi Handicaps. They hoped it was the last.

Auchinleck's victory in the Western Desert was hailed by the people in Britain and America. It was the only bit of good news in a time of gloom for the Allies. Although the German invasion of Russia had been stopped at the gates of Moscow, the Soviet Union was still in grave danger. The Nazi armies held half of European Russia. And on December 7 the Japanese had brought themselves and the United States into the war by attacking Pearl Harbor and destroying most of the American Pacific Fleet. A few days later Japanese airplanes had sunk two powerful British battleships near Singapore, and Japanese soldiers had begun a rapid conquest of Southeast Asia and the nearby Pacific islands.

The British and American governments hoped that Auchinleck would destroy Rommel's army before long so that he and his soldiers could be sent to turn the tide of Axis successes elsewhere. But it was not to be that easy. No one knew it — except possibly Rommel — but there would soon be another running of the Benghazi Handicaps.

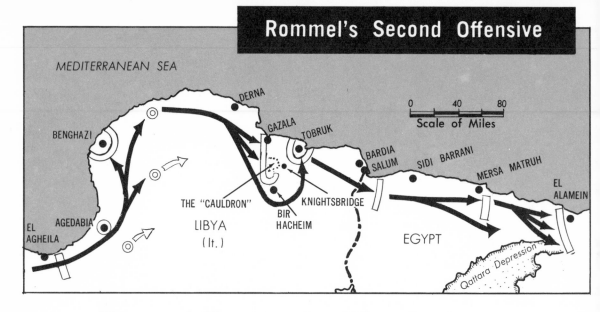

MEDITERRANEAN SEA

DERNA

BENGHAZI

GAZALA

TOBRUK

BARDIA
SALUM

SIDI BARRANI

MERSA MATRUH

EL
ALAMEIN

THE "CAULDRON"

KNIGHTSBRIDGE

BIR
HACHEIM

LIBYA
(It.)

EGYPT

EL
AGHEILA

AGEDABIA

Qattara Depression

0   40   80
Scale of Miles

Rommel Renews the "Benghazi Handicaps"

Buildup at El Agheila

Rommel's defensive position at El Agheila was a strong one. Auchinleck could not send his tanks around the southern flank, as he had done before. A vast swamp, extending inland for many miles, protected the right flank of the Italo-German army. The British had moved so fast from Egypt that Auchinleck could not make a full-scale direct attack on the powerful Axis positions until he could assemble reserves and gather large quantities of ammunition and other supplies.

Both sides began building up their strength as quickly as possible. It was easier for Rommel to do this, because he was closer to his main base at Tripoli than Auchinleck was to his base at Suez. Furthermore, the British were still busy with the sieges of Bardia and Salum. It was not until these Axis fortresses surrendered on January 17, 1942, that Auchinleck was able to send all his troops to El Agheila. Meanwhile, Hitler had finally listened to Rommel's appeals, and had sent supplies and reinforcements. These had arrived in Tripoli earlier in January. Consequently, Rommel was ready for action while Auchinleck was still waiting for his convoys to arrive from Egypt.

Rommel's Second Offensive

ON JANUARY 21 Rommel attacked strongly on a narrow front. The Eighth Army, not yet ready for a major battle, was unable to stop the powerful German drive, and Auchinleck ordered a retreat. At the same time he gave orders for his rear-area troops to build up a new defensive position at Gazala, about forty miles west of Tobruk.

Rommel's advance was so rapid that he overran and captured British dumps of fuel and equipment before the defenders could send these back to the supply depots or destroy them. Using the captured supplies, Rommel was able to feed and re-equip his army without pausing. Before the end of January he had captured Benghazi and its British garrison. Continuing along the coastal road and across the desert further inland, he reached Auchinleck's new defensive line on February 4. There he was forced to halt. The British defenses were weak and thinly manned, but the Germans had advanced so far in so short a time that they had to pause to reorganize before they could mount a full-scale attack.

Again both sides built up their strength feverishly. This time both sides were almost equally distant from their bases, and so, for more than three months, neither side seemed to be gaining an advantage. Except for the superiority of the Royal Navy on the Mediterranean and of the Royal Air Force in the skies over the North African coast, the stalemate might have gone on indefinitely.

As it was, British ships and planes attacked German and Italian supply ships at sea and in harbors in North Africa and Italy. Time after time they bombarded ports where ships were loading in Europe, or unloading in Africa. The main base of these naval and air attacks on Axis shipping was the tiny British island of Malta. This "unsinkable aircraft carrier" defied repeated German bombing attacks.

At the same time, Royal Air Force units based behind the British Gazala line ranged far westward over Cyrenaica, repeatedly hitting German and Italian supply dumps and reserves of fuel, bombing and strafing Axis truck convoys moving along the roads.

Meanwhile, Auchinleck and the new field commander of the Eighth Army — General Neil Ritchie — were building up a powerful line of fortifications for forty miles inland from Gazala, on the coast, to Bir Hacheim. These defenses consisted of a series of entrenchments surrounded by barbed wire, with deep minefields covering the front and connecting each strong point.

Manning the left flank of the Eighth Army position was a contingent of Free French soldiers. These were men who had been in French colonial garrisons in Africa, but who refused to serve under

Smoke billows from an Allied munitions carrier hit behind the battle front in Tunisia by raiding Stuka bombers.

the pro-Nazi Vichy government. Most of these men had made a long, dreary march over the Sahara Desert from central Africa to join the British.

By late May, Rommel realized that British strength was growing faster than his. He had built up his army to about 113,000 men, 560 tanks, and 50 aircraft, but more than half of his men, and 240 of his tanks, were Italian. He did not consider the Italian troops as reliable as his Germans. The British Eighth Army now had more than 125,000 men, 740 tanks, and over 700 aircraft. Furthermore, Rommel knew that at least 200 more British tanks were on their way to the front. He decided to attack before the British strength could grow any greater.

Battle of Knightsbridge-Gazala-Bir Hacheim

ON THE NIGHT of May 27-28, Rommel's Italian troops attacked all along the front of the British fortifications from Gazala to Bir Hacheim. At the same time he personally led the three German divisions of his *Afrika Korps* on a wide sweep around and behind the British left flank. General Ritchie immediately moved British reserves to meet the *panzer* thrust. Now, behind the main British defensive line, a great series of tank battles took place between a road junction called Knightsbridge and the little village of El Adem. Rommel's efforts to move supplies along a route far around the British left flank, were seriously hampered by the air attacks of the Royal Air Force.

Despite the boldness and power of his attacks, Rommel soon realized that he would not gain the quick victory he had hoped for. Most of the British and Free French units continued to hold firm in the main line from Gazala to Bir Hacheim despite the tank battles around Knightsbridge to their rear. Rommel was running short of fuel, food, and ammunition, and at the same time he was losing many tanks.

Nevertheless, Rommel knew that his attacks, and the effective use of his Eighty-eights, had seriously hurt the British. In fact, their tank losses were even greater than his own. On May 30, therefore, he began to carry out one of the most unusual plans in the history of warfare.

Combined German and Italian attacks had hacked their way through the center of the British line. Instead of returning around the southern end of the British line at Bir Hacheim, Rommel withdrew westward as far as the gap in the British line. By June 2 he had established his *Afrika Korps* in a defensive position behind and in the middle of the British fortified area. Instead of a long, vulnerable supply line around the British flank, he could now supply his *Afrika Korps* directly through the gap his troops had cut in the British lines.

Auchinleck's men immediately began a series of violent assaults on this German position deep inside their lines. Because of the fierceness of the fights that swirled around this area, the British called the place the "Cauldron." Holding off the British with his Eighty-eights, Rommel now began to pound the isolated British and Free French positions at Bir Hacheim. For ten days the violent battle raged east and south of the exposed *Afrika Korps'* Cauldron, but by June 11, Rommel finally succeeded in taking the position of Bir Hacheim.

Once more Rommel seized the offensive, and another series of tank battles took place around Knightsbridge. Time and again the Germans lured the British tanks into ambushes where they were shot up by the Eighty-eights. By evening of June 13, the British had only 65 tanks left, out of more than 900 that they had used during the battle. The Germans reached the coast east of Tobruk. The defeated British Eighth Army streamed eastward toward Egypt.

Rommel now concentrated everything he had against Tobruk. By June 19 he had surrounded the city once more. On June 20, he hammered the defenses with artillery and all of his dive bombers. On June 21, the entire *Afrika Korps* charged over the British entrenchments and into the city. Tobruk, so long a symbol of British resistance, was now in Rommel's possession, along with large quantities of fuel and supplies.

Without giving his tired troops a moment's rest, Rommel now dashed eastward along the coastal road and across the desert into Egypt in pursuit of the retreating British Eighth Army. At Mersa Matruh he caught up with the British rear guard, which on June 28 fought a skillful delaying action to slow down the German advance. Rommel, recognizing that the British, despite the loss of 80,000 men, had begun to recover from their defeat, now advanced more cautiously, under constant attack from British aircraft.

Auchinleck had been amazingly successful in restoring order in the shattered Eighth Army. While his rear guard and the Royal Air Force were delaying Rommel's advance, he had established a new defensive line extending south from El Alamein to the forbidding Qattara Depression — a sand sea impassable for large forces. When

An Allied freighter off the coast of North Africa explodes after a direct hit from a German bomber.

Rommel's leading tanks probed against this line on June 30, the British turned them back easily.

By July 7, Rommel had gathered his entire army opposite El Alamein. His probing attacks, however, soon proved to him that he would not be able to get past Auchinleck's new line without a major attack. His army exhausted and badly in need of reorganization, he dug a line of entrenchments opposite the British and sent back for supplies and reinforcements.

Once again the two armies began a race to build up strength for a new attack. Rommel's amazing series of victories gave him and his proud German *Afrika Korps* confidence that they would be able to win again. This time they expected to break through to the Nile River and the Suez Canal. Alexandria was only sixty miles away.

But this meant that the British supply line from El Alamein to Suez was short, and supplies reached the Eighth Army quickly. The British government and the United States were rushing all manner of equipment and reinforcements to threatened Egypt. Winston Churchill himself was flying to the Middle East to encourage his generals and troops in a desperate last-ditch defense.

Destroyed German Mark III tank in Tunisia.

El Alamein

New British Command Team

DURING the month of July, Auchinleck and Rommel hastily reorganized and built up their battle-weary forces. Both made a number of limited attacks to probe and to test each other's strength. Rommel's victorious, confident troops were ready for battle more quickly. The British were able to assemble larger forces, but by this time the discouraged men of the Eighth Army had decided that they could never get the best of wily Rommel, even if they outnumbered his army.

Churchill urged an immediate attack against the Italo-German army, but Auchinleck replied that his men were not ready. So, early in August, 1942, Churchill — despite his admiration for the fine job Auchinleck had done — decided that a new commander was needed for the British in the Middle East.

The new Middle East commander was General Harold Alexander, who had done well commanding a division in France in 1940, and as the commander of British forces in Burma early in 1942. Under him was Lieutenant General Bernard L. Montgomery, who was appointed to command the Eighth Army.

Although Alexander and Montgomery both agreed with Auchinleck that their troops were not yet ready to attack, they made many sweeping changes in the organization of the British forces. Montgomery lost no .opportunity to show his men how confident he was of victory. Under his inspiration, the Eighth Army soon began to feel that perhaps it could fight and beat Rommel and his *Afrika Korps*, after all.

Rommel could sense the growing readiness of the British army. He begged Hitler for more men and more supplies — particularly gasoline

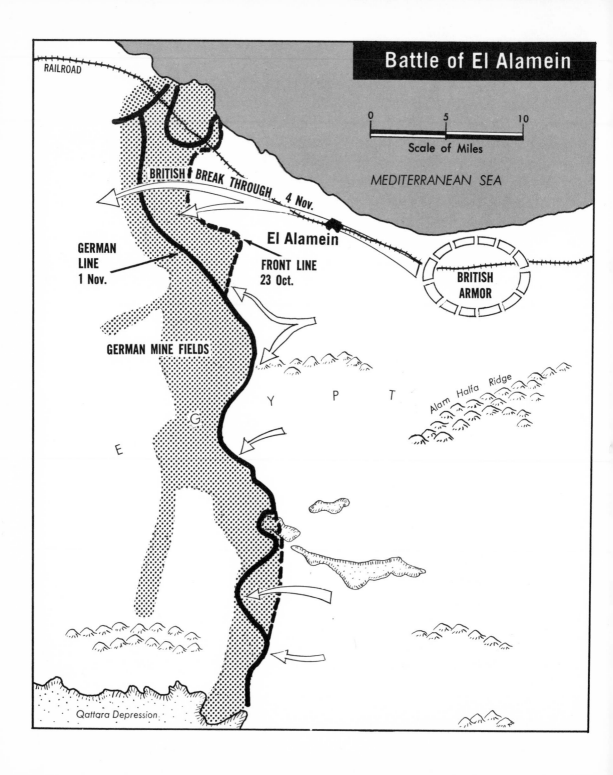

RAILROAD

Battle of El Alamein

0   5   10
Scale of Miles

MEDITERRANEAN SEA

BRITISH BREAK THROUGH 4 Nov.

El Alamein

GERMAN
LINE
1 Nov.

FRONT LINE
23 Oct.

BRITISH
ARMOR

GERMAN MINE FIELDS

E   G   Y   P   T

Alam Halfa Ridge

Qattara Depression

General Bernard L. Montgomery.

for his tanks. Hitler made many promises, but few reinforcements and little fuel arrived. All of Germany's strength was being poured into the great battles in the Russian Caucasus and in front of Stalingrad. Finally Rommel felt that if he did not strike immediately, he would never have another chance to beat the British before they got too strong.

Battle of Alam Halfa

THE BRITISH line in front of El Alamein stretched for 35 miles south from the coast to the Qattara Depression. Several lines of entrenchments were covered by barbed wire and large minefields. But British forces were weak in the south, just north of the Qattara Depression. Rommel decided to try to break through there, and to swing around behind the main British positions, just as he had done to win his great victory at the Gazala line.

Montgomery expected Rommel to attack first, and realized what the German plan would probably be. He did not think that he could keep Rommel from breaking through in the south, but he did believe he could stop the Germans from getting behind the main battle position, as they had done at Knightsbridge.

Immediately behind the center of the British line lay a long hill, called the Alam Halfa Ridge. Montgomery fortified that ridge strongly with artillery, entrenched infantry, and tanks dug into the hill so that only their long guns poked out over the rocks and sand. His calm and careful preparations made his men confident of victory.

Rommel launched his attack on August 31. While the Italians kept the British busy along the front, the *Afrika Korps* smashed ahead in a powerful attack just north of the Qattara Depression. After a tough fight, the Germans finally forced their way through the barbed wire and minefields, then turned northward toward the coast, expecting to cut off the main British battle position. But suddenly they found themselves faced by Montgomery's reserve position along the Alam Halfa Ridge. Despite repeated efforts to break through, the *Afrika Korps* was completely stopped. It was running short of fuel, now, and suffering terribly from British air attacks. Realizing that he could not capture the Alam Halfa Ridge, Rommel admitted defeat. On September 2 his troops began to fight their way back, the way they had come, to their positions opposite El Alamein.

Rommel now realized that his own army was in great danger. He started to pull back into Libya so as to get closer to his own supply base, and to draw the British away from theirs. But he got orders from Hitler not to abandon any territory. Accordingly, he began to strengthen his position by building additional lines of entrenchments, barbed wire, and minefields, in hopes that he could stop the British, just as they had stopped him. He and his men remembered that they had been in dangerous situations before, and had still won through to victory. He made every possible preparation, to try to do it again.

36

Battle of El Alamein

FOR MORE than a month Alexander and Montgomery continued to assemble troops, equipment, and supplies, and to do everything possible to assure a successful attack. Montgomery had worked out a detailed battle plan. Behind the main line he made his soldiers rehearse the plan time and again, just to make sure that every man knew exactly what he was supposed to do. Finally, after the middle of October, he felt he was ready. By this time the British outnumbered the Germans and Italians by more than two to one.

The battle began during the evening of October 23 with a tremendous artillery and air bombardment of the German and Italian positions. That same night, after delivering the heaviest pounding that had ever taken place on the desert, the British attacked.

The next ten days saw the most intense, costly fighting of the entire war in North Africa. Rommel proved that he was just as good a general on the defensive as on the offensive. Despite the great numerical superiority of the British, despite his shortages of fuel and

Allied troops advance past wrecked German vehicles.

other supplies, he counterattacked repeatedly and successfully, inflicting terrible losses on the British.

But Rommel was taking serious losses himself. Even with his skillful use of the Eighty-eights and his *panzer* divisions, he was losing large numbers of his guns and his tanks to the stubborn British, who refused to stop. British air superiority was causing heavy casualties in all German and Italian units, and was preventing supplies from reaching the frontline troops.

Finally, on November 2, the British broke through the deep Axis defensive position, and Rommel knew the battle was lost. He ordered an immediate withdrawal, but again Hitler ordered him not to abandon any territory. For one more day Rommel tried to hold on, but his losses were so great that he knew any further delay would mean the loss of his entire army. On November 4, despite Hitler's orders, he again began to withdraw. The Battle of El Alamein was over.

El Alamein was one of the decisive battles of World War II. It ended the last Axis threat to British control of the Middle East. From that time on Axis power in the Mediterranean steadily declined, while that of the Allies increased. El Alamein, combined with the simultaneous successful Russian defense at Stalingrad, was a turning point in the war.

Last Running of the "Benghazi Handicaps"

WITH his usual skill, Rommel began a rapid withdrawal from Egypt. He knew he could not save his Italian infantry divisions south of the British breakthrough, so he ruthlessly sacrificed them to hold up the British advance as well as they could, while he pulled back with the *Afrika Korps* and a few of his Italian tank units.

Montgomery pushed energetically after the retreating Germans, assisted greatly by the air strikes of the Royal Air Force. Rommel's

American-built tanks on the way to the front in the British Eighth Army's advance to Tripoli.

remaining forces suffered terribly, and were forced to abandon most of their tanks and heavy weapons. Both the victorious British general and the defeated German deserve great credit for the vigorous efforts each made at this time. Though Montgomery came close to cutting the Germans off, he never quite made it. And although

Rommel finally forced his way out of the trap, his army lost all of its fighting capability as it fled westward into Libya and past Benghazi.

Rommel received a few reinforcements and some supplies at El Agheila, where he had started his first offensive. He halted briefly there on November 23. Montgomery rushed up three divisions, collected a few supplies, and attacked on December 11. After a two-day fight, Rommel was forced to retreat again. He held up the British briefly for two weeks in late December and early January, 1943, while Montgomery's troops were waiting for their supply trucks to catch up. Then, on January 23, the British advanced again — this time to Tripoli, capital of Libya.

When Montgomery arrived in Tripoli, he was met by some unexpected reinforcements. These were Free French soldiers from Equatorial Africa, led by brilliant young General Jean Leclerc. Leclerc and his men had long before revolted from the Vichy government, and had maintained themselves at Fort Lamy, near Lake Chad. They had been raiding Italian outposts in the Sahara in southern Libya when they learned of the Battle of El Alamein. In December, 1942, Leclerc had led his men northward on a 1600-mile march across the desert, capturing several Italian posts on the way. After a thirty-nine day campaign they reached Tripoli, just as the Eighth Army was arriving.

Continuing without pause, Montgomery pushed on into southern Tunisia after the fleeing Rommel. But here, early in February, the British were forced to halt. Rommel had finally gathered enough troops to create an effective defensive position at Mareth. Here the longest, fastest — and last — running of the Benghazi Handicaps came to an end. The war in North Africa entered a new phase, but it was far from ended.

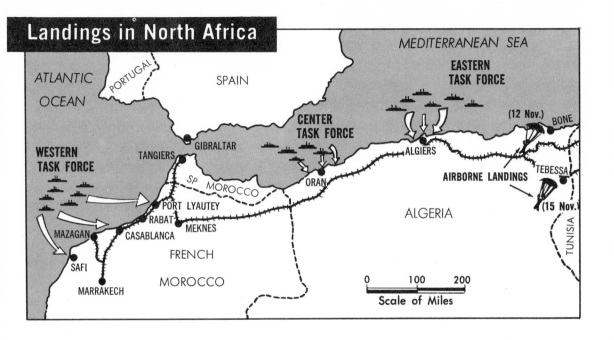

Landings in North Africa

Operation TORCH

Hitler's New Strategy in Africa

ONE REASON for Rommel's inability to assemble forces enough to keep Montgomery from capturing Tripoli was the series of events taking place in northwest Africa. On November 8, 1942, British and American troops had landed at three places in Morocco and Algeria. All of the German and Italian troops that could be rushed to Africa were needed to meet this new threat to the Axis position in the Mediterranean.

41

Up until this time the Germans and Italians had been able to fight the British in the Middle East without any worries about the security of their Libyan base. Morocco, Algeria, and Tunisia in northwest Africa were French possessions, under the administration of the Vichy government of France. That government was controlled by Adolf Hitler, and so German-dominated Vichy-French soldiers protected the approaches to Rommel's base area from the west and northwest.

But when Allied troops landed in Morocco and Algeria, Hitler's grip on the French colonies in North Africa suddenly began to weaken. The unprotected rear areas and supply bases of Rommel's army were threatened. The entire Axis position on the south shore of the Mediterranean was in terrible danger.

But Hitler knew that if he could keep German troops in northeastern Tunisia, and Italian forces in Sicily, Allied ships would not be able to use the narrow Sicilian Channel. This would mean that the Allies would not be able to gain control of the Mediterranean. Hitler therefore began to rush great quantities of German troops to Tunisia, and he ordered Rommel to fall back and hold the region at all costs.

Tunisia was a mountainous country, easy to defend. Hitler had persuaded himself that a brilliant general like Rommel could stop the Allies there, and then use the area as a base from which to reconquer all of North Africa.

The Allied Strategy in North Africa

THE ALLIES had decided to make their landings in Morocco and Algeria for several reasons. Most important was the desire of both President Roosevelt and Prime Minister Churchill to get started on the long task of smashing down the armed might of Germany. They

American troops land at Surcouf, near Algiers.

knew that although their own peoples were impatient to get the war
over with, it takes a long time to build up great armies. At that moment, neither the British nor the American forces were ready to attack the Germans directly in Europe.

Like Hitler, they realized that if they could drive the Axis powers
from North Africa, Allied naval forces could gain control over the
Mediterranean Sea. Also, from bases in Africa it would be possible
to attack Italy and German-controlled France from the south. This
would mean that the Germans would have to transfer some of their
troops from Russia to western Europe. This would help the Russians

43

to recover from the terrible blows that they had suffered from Hitler's attacks in 1941 and 1942. Furthermore, if Vichy-French control of North Africa could be broken, the Free French forces of General Charles de Gaulle could establish themselves on French territory and gain recruits from the large French population of the North African colonies.

The Allies knew, however, that there was a grave risk in invading Algeria and Morocco. The Vichy government was firmly under the control of Hitler, and there was a great danger that French troops in Africa would fight fiercely against the Allied landings. Tragically, many Frenchmen would be killed fighting for Germany, and they would at the same time kill many Americans and British who merely wanted to liberate France from the tyrannical rule of Hitler's Nazis.

To try to prevent this, a group of American officers, under Major General Mark W. Clark, were brought to the coast of Algeria by submarine in late October. They went ashore in small rubber boats. There they met secretly with a group of French officers who wanted to break away from German control and re-establish a truly free France.

The daring conspirators were discovered by Nazi-controlled French police, but all managed to escape. The Americans swam out to their submarine, and the French officers slipped back to their units. Although the meeting was not finished, and only partly successful, the Americans now realized that many Frenchmen would join the Allies if they had the chance.

The Landings

ON NOVEMBER 6, 1942, an American lieutenant general flew from London to Gibraltar to establish a new Anglo-American headquar-

44

ters. His name was Dwight D. Eisenhower; his mission was to lead Allied forces in Operation TORCH — an invasion of French Morocco and Algeria. The forces under Eisenhower's command were at sea in three great convoys of transports, escorted by powerful American and British naval units. Early that same morning, two of these convoys — coming from England — had secretly entered the Mediterranean by passing through the Straits of Gibraltar.

In the lead was the Eastern Task Force, commanded by American Major General Charles W. Ryder. It consisted of 33,000 men, about half American and half British, and was escorted by twenty-two British warships. The mission of the Eastern Task Force was to capture the seaport of Algiers, capital city of Algeria.

Close behind the Eastern Task Force came the Center Task Force, heading for Oran, second largest city of Algeria. In command was American Major General Lloyd R. Fredendall, who had a force of 39,000 troops, all American. The Center Task Force was escorted by twenty-one British warships.

Out on the Atlantic was a third convoy: the Western Task Force, commanded by Major General George S. Patton, Jr. This force of 35,000 American troops had sailed directly from the United States, and was escorted by forty-seven American warships. The Western Task Force was to make its main landings near Casablanca, the prin-

Men, munitions, and supplies are unloaded by British and United States forces in Algiers.

General George S. Patton.

cipal city of Morocco. Smaller landings were to be made at Port Lyautey, about 70 miles north of Casablanca, and at Safi, some 125 miles to the south.

Right on schedule, before dawn on November 8, all three task forces began their landings.

At Algiers, where the most difficulty had been expected, the Allies had the least trouble. Aided by a few French troops who declared for General de Gaulle, the Eastern Task Force quickly overcame Vichy-French resistance, even though one landing attempt at the city waterfront was repelled. Admiral Jean F. Darlan, commander of all the Vichy armed forces, happened to be in Algiers at the time. As Allied forces closed in on the city soon after dark on November 8, Darlan ordered his troops to surrender.

The fighting lasted longer at Oran. The assault troops, landing on both sides of the city, began a two-pronged envelopment, but soon ran into stiff Vichy-French resistance that held up the advance all day. Just before dawn, a small naval landing force tried to seize Oran harbor by surprise, but the French naval harbor defense force was alert. It smashed the two American light vessels with point-blank gunfire. The survivors were forced to surrender.

Soon after this, airplanes carrying British and American paratroopers arrived from England to capture the main airfield near Oran. But a storm had blown the planes off course, and by mistake the paratroopers were dropped twenty miles away from their objective.

Next day the fighting around Oran continued, with the French attempting some counterattacks against the Americans. These were repulsed, however, and the invaders pressed so close to the city that they were able to capture the outlying airfields. Early on November 10, the advance continued into the outskirts of the city, and Admiral Darlan sent a radio message from Algiers, ordering the defenders to surrender. They gave up shortly after noon, just as the Americans were preparing to make a final assault.

The hardest fighting of Operation TORCH took place along the Moroccan coast. Safi was captured quickly, but fighting around Casablanca and Port Lyautey was fierce. At both of these places, the soldiers were greatly assisted in capturing the beaches by the accurate gunfire of supporting U.S. Navy ships. But the French navy performed almost equally well, and it came close to ruining the American landings. French destroyers dashed out of Casablanca to attack invading soldiers and ships, but they were finally beaten back by the American warships.

Not until late on November 9 were the beachheads near Port Lyautey and Casablanca secure. On November 10, the American invaders began to advance into both Casablanca and Port Lyautey. By evening of that day the French defenders were close to defeat, and that night they received orders from Darlan to surrender. Early on the morning of November 11, French troops in Morocco capitulated to the Americans.

Operation TORCH had succeeded.

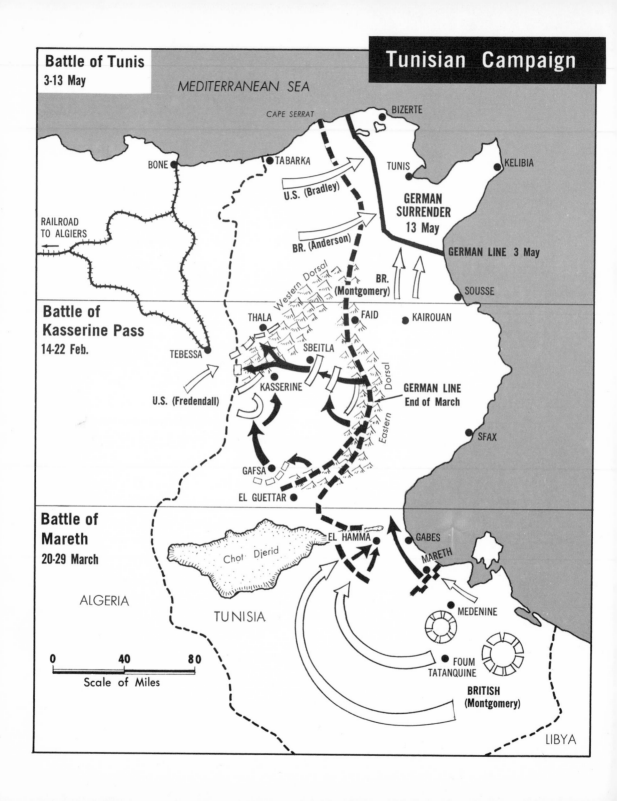

Battle of Tunis
3-13 May

MEDITERRANEAN SEA

Tunisian Campaign

CAPE SERRAT

BIZERTE

BONE

TABARKA

TUNIS

KELIBIA

U.S. (Bradley)

GERMAN
SURRENDER
13 May

BR. (Anderson)

GERMAN LINE 3 May

RAILROAD
TO ALGIERS

BR.
(Montgomery)

SOUSSE

Western Dorsal

**Battle of
Kasserine Pass**
14-22 Feb.

THALA

FAID

KAIROUAN

TEBESSA

SBEITLA

Eastern Dorsal

KASSERINE

GERMAN LINE
End of March

U.S. (Fredendall)

SFAX

GAFSA

EL GUETTAR

**Battle of
Mareth**
20-29 March

Chot Djerid

EL HAMMA

GABES

MARETH

ALGERIA

TUNISIA

MEDENINE

0   40   80

Scale of Miles

FOUM
TATANQUINE

BRITISH
(Montgomery)

LIBYA

Tunisia

The Race for Tunis

As EARLY AS November 9, Hitler had begun to rush troops to Tunisia in accordance with his new strategic plan for a desperate, last-ditch defense in North Africa. The next day British and American troops also began to race eastward toward Tunis by land, sea and air.

Additional Allied troops began to arrive rapidly in Algeria. The British were organized as the First British Army, under the immediate command of British General Kenneth Anderson. General Eisenhower, moving to Algiers from Gibraltar, ordered Anderson to try to seize the key Tunisian cities of Tunis and Bizerte as rapidly as possible. General Fredendall, commanding the American II Corps, was to advance on Anderson's right, from Tebessa, in eastern Algeria.

Meanwhile, General Mark Clark was placed in overall command of the remaining American troops in Morocco and western Algeria. These were organized into the new American Fifth Army, and were prepared to march north into Spanish Morocco if Spanish dictator Francisco Franco interfered, or if German troops tried to move south through Spain. But Franco, impressed by the efficiency and success of Operation TORCH, remained neutral, and so General Clark's army began to prepare for further operations in the Mediterranean area as soon as Tunisia was captured by the Allies.

But that conquest was proving to be a much harder task than had been expected. Although General Anderson's troops were advancing eastward as rapidly as they could, Hitler was rushing large numbers of his very best troops to Tunis and Bizerte by sea and by air. Hard fighting between isolated German and Allied columns began in north central Tunisia as early as November 17. Although the Allies had a

49

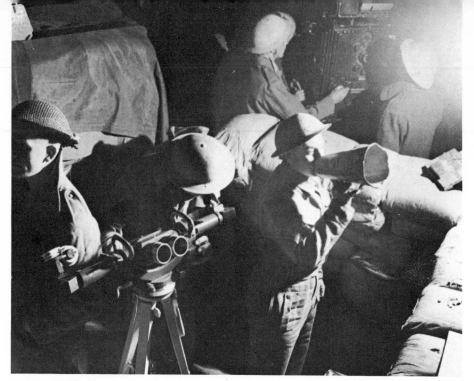

Allied command post in action near Benghazi, North Africa.

head start, the Germans had a shorter distance to move from Sicily and Italy, and they were able to make good use of the rugged, easily defended mountains of Tunisia. The Allies, who had not yet had time to build a supply base in Algeria, were short of trucks, tanks and other equipment.

Hitler organized his troops in Tunis as the Fifth *Panzer* Army and placed General Juergen von Arnim in command. Taking advantage of the weakness of the advancing Allied columns, von Arnim's counterattacks soon had the Allies on the defensive in several places in northern and central Tunisia. General Eisenhower rushed reinforcements to the front as soon as they arrived by ship in Algeria, however, and by November 28 two small Allied columns had pushed to within twenty miles of Tunis.

Von Arnim now counterattacked strongly and threw the Allies back more than twenty miles. Here the German advance was halted by more Allied reinforcements. During the month of December a stalemate spread over the opposing positions. The line ran roughly south through the mountains of Tunisia from the Mediterranean Sea — near Cape Serrat — along the Eastern Dorsal Range as far south as Gafsa and El Guettar. Both Eisenhower and von Arnim remained on the defensive as they built up their forces for further operations early in 1943.

Stalemate in Tunisia

THE GERMANS had won the race for Tunis, but they knew that their situation was dangerous, since they held only a narrow strip of eastern Tunisia. Hitler continued to rush troops to von Arnim, and ordered Rommel — still retreating from El Alamein — to withdraw his shattered army into southern Tunisia.

Rommel arrived near Mareth early in January. During his retreat from El Alamein he had performed marvels in reorganizing his bat-

The British Eighth Army moves in on Tripoli.

tered army, and had been able to re-equip it from the supply depots in Tripoli as he passed through. He immediately set to work to build a powerful defensive position. This reached from the sea, near Mareth, several miles inland into the desert. When the leading troops of Montgomery's Eighth Army arrived near Mareth on February 15, they found themselves faced by a powerful line of German entrenchments. Here the long British pursuit ended, almost 1500 miles west of the battlefield of El Alamein — one of the longest pursuits in military history, and a credit both to the pursuer and to the pursued.

Meanwhile Rommel — traveling by light airplane, automobile, and tank — had made a quick but thorough survey of the Allied front lines in southern Tunisia. He returned convinced that a powerful, coordinated German attack could smash the American and French troops in Tunisia before Montgomery's army could interfere.

What Rommel had seen had made him think that the Allies were poorly organized and confused. And he had been quite right. General Anderson's First Army consisted of the British V Corps in the north, the small French XIX Corps in the center (opposite Kairouan), and Fredendall's American II Corps in the south. The command relationship between Anderson and his French and American corps commanders was not clear. Both commanders seemed to think they should be directly under General Eisenhower, even though he had ordered them under Anderson's command late in January.

The situation within the Allied contingents was also confused, except for the experienced British veterans in the north. Von Arnim had been able to take advantage of the inexperience and disorganization within the French and American corps by a number of successful small attacks in January and early February.

Now Rommel informed Hitler and von Arnim of his own estimate, and suggested an immediate joint attack by his own *panzer* and

The British Eighth Army finds it hard going over the road between Homs and Tripoli.

motorized divisions and von Arnim's Fifth Army. Leaving a few Italian and German infantry troops to hold the line at Mareth, Rommel promptly began his preparations for the attack.

At this time Hitler made a very serious mistake. It caused almost as much confusion in German forces in Tunisia as existed in the Allied First Army. Instead of putting von Arnim under Rommel's command, he kept the two German armies separate. Von Arnim was a good, workmanlike German general, but he lacked the brilliance, skill, and energy of Rommel. He agreed to join in an attack against the American II Corps, but he did not coordinate his plans closely with Rommel, and he did not put as large a force into the attack as Rommel believed he should have. Nevertheless, Rommel went ahead with his own plan.

Battle of Kasserine Pass

ON FEBRUARY 14 — Saint Valentine's Day — Rommel struck against the American II Corps in the kind of surprise attack that had caused so much trouble to veteran British troops in the Western Desert. On a broad front, from Faid to El Guettar, the German *panzers* swept through the passes of the Eastern Dorsal Range into the broad valley between that range and the Western Dorsal Mountains.

The German tanks brushed aside the American outposts at Gafsa and west of Faid and dashed toward Sbeitla and Kasserine. The Americans had been learning about war during the fighting of the previous months, but they had never experienced anything like this brilliantly planned and brilliantly performed attack. Several units were completely smashed. The survivors were captured by the Germans.

General Fredendall pulled back his advanced units nevertheless, and hastily reorganized his forces to defend the passes of the Western Dorsal Range. And despite confusion, surprise, and shock, his troops performed well. But they simply lacked the experience and sound combat leadership to stop Rommel's attack. Furthermore, due to confusion back in Eisenhower's Allied Force headquarters, British and American air units were spread out over the entire front, instead of concentrating against Rommel's main threat, as they should have been.

On February 18 Rommel seized Kasserine, and continued on to Kasserine Pass. There he was held up for a day and a half by the really heroic resistance of a few scattered American infantry and artillery units. But the veteran *Afrika Korps* infantrymen, riding up in their trucks, swung into action beside their tanks, enveloped the American defenders of the pass, and threw them back. The German

54

tanks raced on, and by February 22 were within twenty miles of Tebessa, in eastern Algeria, the main supply point and communications center for Allied troops in southern and central Tunisia. If Tebessa had fallen, the entire Allied position in Tunisia would have been threatened. The Allies probably would have had to withdraw to Algeria.

But now Rommel was forced to stop. The main reason was that von Arnim had failed to make any really important attack while Rommel had been driving forward. As a result General Anderson was able to release part of the American First Armored Division, which had been in reserve, and had also been able to draw some British units out of the line in the north. These reserve units joined with the hard-pressed Americans east and northeast of Tebessa to halt the German advance. At the same time Allied airplanes began to concentrate against Rommel.

The German general realized that without help from von Arnim he could get no further. Short of fuel, his supply lines and combat troops pounded from the air, he had no choice but to withdraw. With his customary brilliance and skill he disengaged his leading elements. Leaving a methodically planted minefield behind him, he returned to the coastal plain as quickly as he had advanced.

Rommel had severely punished the American troops, and he had possibly gained nearly a month by forcing the Allies to reorganize and to postpone their planned offensive. But, having failed to smash the Allies completely — as might have happened if von Arnim had cooperated — Rommel had also done them some unintended favors.

Rommel had shown the inexperienced Americans how a master of war conducts *blitzkrieg*. This was a lesson they would never forget, and which they would later use very effectively against him. He had also forced Eisenhower to completely reorganize and improve the

Tunisia, North Africa. General Dwight D. Eisenhower and General George Patton examine a map in General Patton's office.

Allied command system for later operations in Tunisia. And he had made the British and Americans work out an effective method for using air power in support of ground troops; a method that would be used successfully by the Allies throughout the remainder of the war.

Final Battles in Tunisia

DURING late February and early March, General Eisenhower reorganized his forces in preparation for a powerful combined attack against the Germans. His plan was to have the British First Army and American II Corps keep the Germans busy in northern and central Tunisia, while Montgomery's British Eighth Army was making the main attack against Rommel's Mareth Line in southern Tunisia.

Meanwhile Hitler had put Rommel in command of all German forces in Tunisia. Rommel took all possible steps to get his own army and von Arnim's ready for the expected Allied attack.

On March 20, Montgomery's troops attacked the Mareth Line, but were thrown back by the Germans. Montgomery now decided to send part of his army westward into the desert, to try to get around the right flank of the Mareth Line. At the same time, the American II Corps — now commanded by Major General George Patton — attacked southeast from Gafsa against the right rear of the German positions in southern Tunisia.

Aerial view of a German prisoner-of-war camp west of Mateur, North Africa. The Allies took nearly 9,000 German prisoners in a single day.

This combined attack threatened to cut off the outnumbered Germans. Rommel withdrew from his positions near Mareth and retreated northward, to link his army more closely with that of von Arnim in northeastern Tunisia. Soon after this, however, he became seriously ill, and was ordered back to Germany. Von Arnim took his place as commander of Axis forces in Tunisia.

General Patton had done such a fine job in his attacks against Rommel from Gafsa that he was promoted and given command of the newly formed American Seventh Army in Algeria. There he began to get ready for another great invasion, to take place as soon as the Allies conquered Tunisia. To replace Patton, Major General Omar Bradley was put in command of the II Corps.

Now General Eisenhower prepared for a final effort in Tunisia. He ordered Bradley's II Corps to the northern end of the line, opposite the Tunisian city of Bizerte. This permitted British General Anderson to concentrate his First Army opposite the center of the new German defensive position, near Tunis, capital city of Tunisia. Eisenhower ordered Anderson's army to make the main attack. Montgomery's army and the French XIX Corps, on the right flank, and Bradley's corps, on the left flank, were to assist.

The big attack began on May 3. The Germans put up their usual hard fight, but their lines were soon split by the powerful Allied assaults. On May 7, British tanks dashed into the city of Tunis. That same day Bradley's American troops fought their way into Bizerte.

Von Arnim fought back desperately, but his troops were confused and exhausted. They were soon surrounded by the British and Americans. On May 13, the last Axis defender of Tunisia surrendered. About 275,000 Germans and Italians had been captured during these last ten days of battle in Tunisia.

Now the Allies looked northward to Sicily and Italy.

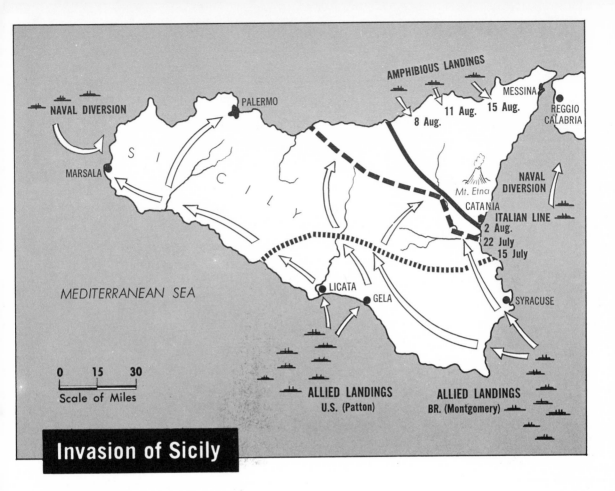

Invasion of Sicily

Sicily

Preparing for Invasion

EVEN before the final Allied assault in Tunisia, the Combined Chiefs of Staff had ordered General Eisenhower to prepare for an invasion of Sicily by the American and British forces under his command.

The location of Sicily made it very important to Allied strategy. The island extends southwestward from Italy to within ninety miles of the coast of Tunisia. Here the Sicilian channel divides the Mediterranean into two basins, east and west. So long as Axis air and submarine forces could be based in Sicily, the Allies could not re-open the "lifeline" from England to Asia, through the Suez Canal.

Sicily was also important to the Allies as a possible steppingstone for further attacks against the Axis in Italy and southern France. The conquest of Tunisia provided the Allies with a number of seaports and air bases from which to mount and support an amphibious attack across the Sicilian channel. And once the island of Sicily was in Allied possession, its seaports and airfields would then be useful for the next short overwater jump to invade Italy itself.

As early as April, General Eisenhower had selected General Montgomery's veteran British Eighth Army and General Patton's newly organized American Seventh Army to carry out Operation HUSKY. This was to be an amphibious invasion of Sicily. The two armies were grouped together as the Fifteenth Army Group, under the over-all direction of General Alexander, who had formerly commanded British forces in the Middle East.

By early July Alexander's army group consisted of 160,000 men, 600 tanks, and 1800 artillery guns. In support were a powerful Anglo-American naval force and almost 3700 American and British air force planes.

U.S. Amphibious "duck trucks" roll ashore in Sicily as U.S. Coast Guard transport disgorges men and materiel for the invasion.

U.S. Liberator bombers blast Messina, Sicilian lifeline to Italy.

The Axis commander in Sicily was Italian General Alfred Guzzoni, with a combined German-Italian force of nearly 200,000 men and 1400 airplanes. About half of this command was German, and it was excellent. The Italian troops, however, were tired of the war, and could not be counted on to fight hard. Furthermore, intensive Allied air attacks on the island in June and early July had still further weakened their enthusiasm.

The Sicilian Landings

THE Allied invasion of Sicily began just before dawn on July 10, 1943. The British Eighth Army struck the southeast corner of the island, just below the city of Syracuse. The American Seventh Army landed a few miles further west, along the south coast, on both sides of the town of Gela. The landings took General Guzzoni completely by surprise. Allied naval activity had tricked him into expecting the attacks to be made against western Sicily.

61

The only serious troubles the Allies ran into at the beginning of the invasion was with their airborne landings. Both American and British paratroops and glider units were blown off course by a storm during the night, and, in the darkness, were scattered all over southern Sicily. Then when later waves of British and American planes came in for more airborne landings, Allied warships and ground troops mistook them for German planes and shot many of them down. Yet despite these difficulties, the paratroopers and glider soldiers fought well and helped establish the beachhead rapidly.

The Germans quickly recovered from their surprise and rushed to attack the Allied beachheads. By July 11 German *panzer* and infantry counterattacks had come very close to pushing the outnumbered American troops back to the seacoast near Gela. But the Germans received little help from the Italians. The Americans rallied and, with the help of fire from warships near the coast, drove the Germans back inland.

In following days more British and American troops poured ashore. By July 15 they had pushed the Italians and Germans completely out of southeastern Sicily. Without pausing, the Allies continued into the mountainous interior of the island. American armored and infantry units swept around the west coast to capture Palermo, capital of Sicily, on July 22.

But German reinforcements began to arrive in Sicily, and the defense was now being handled by one-armed German General Hans Hube, who had distinguished himself in Russia. Making skillful use of the rugged mountains, Hube anchored his left flank on the slopes of the famous volcano, Mt. Etna, and organized a defensive line to hold the northeastern portion of the island.

In late July and early August, the Germans prevented Montgomery's men from making any advance past Mt. Etna. Further

An Allied unit searches for enemy snipers in Messina, Sicily.

An Italian destroyer lies on her side in Palermo Harbor after being sunk by Allied planes.

north and west, however, Patton's Americans inched their way forward despite the determined German defense. Patton forced the German right flank back by several small amphibious landings on the north coast, behind the German front lines.

By mid-August General Hube realized that further resistance on Sicily would mean that his entire army would be cut off, and so he began a well-conducted withdrawal across the narrow Strait of Messina. Despite Allied naval and air attacks, the Germans withdrew across the strait so skillfully that their losses were not serious. By August 17 the last German soldier had retreated to Italy. Most of the Italian soldiers had surrendered, though a few of them had gone with the Germans.

Even more important than the victory itself was the effect that the conquest of the island of Sicily had on Italy. Mussolini's government had lost all popular support. During the middle of the campaign, it collapsed. Mussolini fled to the Germans for protection, and a new Italian government was established with the respected Marshal Pietro Badoglio as prime minister. Badoglio immediately began secret peace negotiations with the Allies. Hitler suspected that Italy was about to desert the Axis cause, and rushed more troops to Italy to try to prevent an Italian surrender, or to occupy the country if Badoglio did give up. Despite this, on September 3 Badoglio secretly agreed to surrender on September 8.

In the next chapter we shall see why September 8 was such an important date to the Allies and to the Italians.

Invasion of Italy

The Invasion of Italy

Allied Strategy for Italy

THE American and British top military commanders — the Combined
Chiefs of Staff — agreed that the best way to keep pressure on the
Axis would be to use Sicily as a steppingstone for an immediate in-
vasion of Italy. This would not give either the Italians or the Germans

time to recover from the terrible defeats they had received in Africa and in Sicily.

The Allied leaders were certain that the Italians would surrender as soon as they knew their country was to be invaded. And if they surrendered, Germany would have to shoulder the entire burden of the defense of Italy. At the same time, additional German troops would be needed to keep the Italian people under control. The only way Hitler could find more divisions would be to take them from the Russian front, where he was already hard pressed by Soviet counteroffensives.

General Eisenhower was ordered to have his Anglo-American forces invade Italy early in September, 1943. As in Sicily, General Alexander was in direct command of the invasion, and as before, Montgomery's British Eighth Army made up half of Alexander's Fifteenth Army Group. The other half was the new American Fifth Army, which had been formed in Morocco and Algeria under General Mark Clark. The troops of General Patton's Seventh Army, who had done so well in Sicily, were ordered to England to prepare for the invasion of northern France in 1944.

The Allied plan for the attack on Italy was like a boxer's one-two punch. Early in September Montgomery's army would cross the Strait of Messina. The Allied planners expected that the Germans would rush troops to the toe of the Italian boot to try to stop Montgomery. Then, a few days later, Clark's army would land further up the west coast of Italy, near Naples, to strike the flank and rear of the Germans facing Montgomery. The two Allied armies would then join in an advance to capture Naples and the east coast town of Foggia. Naples was one of Italy's greatest cities, and the Allies needed its harbor and docks to land supplies. Foggia was important to them because it was a flat region with many airfields, which could be used by Allied bombers to attack southern Germany.

The Combined Chiefs of Staff had not yet decided whether or not Eisenhower's and Alexander's armies should then continue the advance to Rome and northern Italy. They intended to wait and see what happened in Italy after Naples and Foggia were captured.

The Landings in Southern Italy

ACCORDING to plan, Montgomery's veteran British Eighth Army troops crossed the Strait of Messina at dawn on September 3, 1943. The Italians offered no opposition, and at first the British moved forward rapidly. German troops soon arrived, however, to slow down the British advance.

On September 8, the day before General Clark's army was due to land south of Naples, Italy surrendered to the Allies. The Italian fleet sailed out to join the Allies at Malta, and the Italian army prepared to help Eisenhower's men drive the Germans from Italy.

But Hitler and his German commanders in Italy had expected this surrender, and although they had only eight divisions there, they were ready. The German air force attacked the Italian fleet at sea and damaged it severely. At the same time, after a short fight with Italian soldiers there, German troops seized Rome. And in southern Italy, the Germans captured and disarmed all Italian troops and took over their defensive positions. In a few hours the Germans were in

A *destroyer belches a smoke screen to protect a U.S. warship during invasion action at Salerno.*

complete control of all of Italy. This was one of the most remarkable displays of German efficiency during the entire war.

Early on September 9, American and British troops of General Clark's Fifth Army waded ashore at the beaches along the coast of the Gulf of Salerno, about thirty miles south of Naples. Although the landings were successful, the Allies were surprised to find that the Germans had a division near Salerno, ready to meet the attack.

Battle of Salerno

WHAT HAD happened was that the German commander, Field Marshal Kesselring, and his staff had made a careful study of what the Allied plan might be. They figured out that a landing would be made near Naples about a week after Montgomery landed on the toe of the Italian boot. And they studied all of the problems the Allies would have in sending troops to the Naples area, and the difficulties they would have in getting air support from Sicily. The result of this German study came to exactly the same conclusion that had been reached by the Allied staffs of Generals Alexander and Clark: Salerno was the best place for a landing.

So, one German division was hastily sent to defend against an Allied landing at Salerno, and others were alerted to move there just as soon as they could be sure that this was really the main Allied landing. These preparations were another example of German military skill and efficiency.

As a result, the fighting along the beaches near Salerno was bitter and desperate. The Americans and British were able to hold off the determined German counterattacks only with the assistance of nearby Allied warships, and the help of fighter planes based in Sicily. On September 13, and again the next day, the Germans came very close to driving the Allied troops back into the sea.

Mule pack trains carrying supplies to troops fighting in the mountainous regions of Italy. In this rugged terrain mules could travel where wheeled vehicles could not.

But Allied reinforcements were poured into the narrow beachhead by boat, and more were parachuted from airplanes. By September 15, General Clark's force had been built up to a strength equal to that of the Germans, and the general continued to receive reinforcements. Kesselring, however, had no more reinforcements to put into the fight. Furthermore, Montgomery, advancing rapidly from the southern tip of Italy, began to threaten the rear of the Germans around the Salerno beachhead. Reluctantly the Germans began to withdraw.

On September 16 the advancing Eighth Army met the forward troops of the Fifth Army southeast of Salerno. The invasion was now certain of success, but the Allies had learned that they would have to fight very hard to beat the Germans in Italy!

Engineers begin construction of the main Allied Fifth Army pontoon bridge over the Volturno River in Italy.

Sections of the pontoon bridge, to be used for such heavy equipment as trucks and tanks, are put in place.

The Fifth and Eighth armies now began to move north up the Italian peninsula, side by side. The Eighth Army was on the right, between the Apennine Mountains and the Adriatic Sea, advancing toward Foggia. The Fifth Army stayed on the west coast, heading for Naples.

On October 1, the Fifth Army entered Naples, while the Eighth Army was sweeping across the Foggia Plain. A few days later, however, the advances were stopped by strong German defensive positions behind the Volturno River in the west and the Trigno River on the east coast.

From the Volturno to the Winter Line

THE Combined Chiefs of Staff now decided that the advance up the Italian boot should continue. The idea was to keep as many German divisions as possible engaged so that they could not be used against the Russians or to build up the German defenses in northern France, where the next Allied landing was planned for early 1944. Eisenhower, therefore, ordered the advance to continue toward Rome.

Meanwhile, in the more mountainous country just north of the Volturno, Kesselring had been preparing a line of powerful fortifications stretching across the peninsula. This line, which generally followed the line of the Rapido River in the west, and the Sangro River in the east, was called the "Winter Position," or "Winter Line." The western portion of the main German defensive line, the "Gustav Line," between the sea and Cassino, was particularly strong.

When the Allies attacked in mid-October, Kesselring slowly withdrew his forward troops to the fortifications of the Winter Line, which were being strengthened by his engineers and reserve troops. By November 15 all the Germans had pulled back to these positions. The Allies were unable to make any more progress.

71

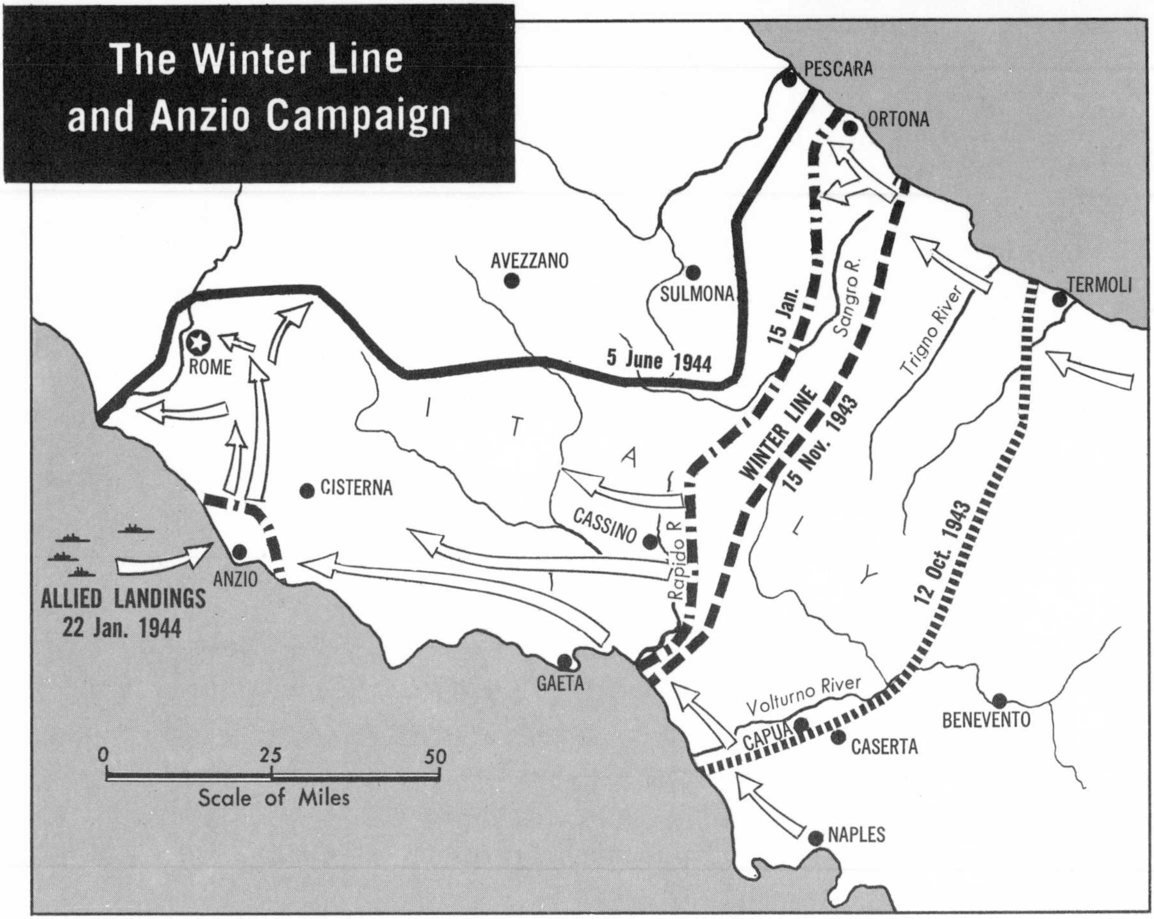
The Winter Line
and Anzio Campaign
PESCARA
ORTONA
AVEZZANO
SULMONA
TERMOLI
ROME
5 June 1944
15 Jan.
Sangro R.
Trigno River
WINTER LINE
15 Nov. 1943
I T A L Y
CISTERNA
CASSINO
Rapido R.
12 Oct. 1943
ANZIO
ALLIED LANDINGS
22 Jan. 1944
GAETA
Volturno River
CAPUA
CASERTA
BENEVENTO
NAPLES
0
25
50
Scale of Miles

The Advance on Rome

The Winter Line Campaign

Soon after Naples was captured, both the American Fifth and British Eighth armies had to send many of their best divisions to England to prepare for the coming invasion of France. They received a number of replacements from England, America, and other Allied countries, but these were new troops with no experience in battle. So, for more than a month, Generals Clark and Montgomery had to stop their attacks against the German entrenchments while they reorganized their armies. Early in November, 1943, General Alexander ordered them to prepare for a new offensive to break through the Winter Line.

The Eighth Army began its attack on November 20. The Fifth Army got started on December 1. Both armies discovered that they could do very little against the strong German defenses. And the weather was terrible. The troops on both sides were miserable as they fought across the cold mountains. The only time the rain stopped, it seemed to the soldiers, was when it changed to snow. Nevertheless, both the Allies and the Germans fought sturdily and courageously.

It finally became obvious to the Allied generals that they could not break through the German lines. They did not have enough troops to overcome the Germans' skillful use of the mountains, and too many of their troops were new recruits, replacing the veterans that had been sent to England. The Eighth Army halted its attacks on December 30; the Fifth Army stopped a few days later. They had hardly dented Kesselring's Winter Line.

By this time there had been several changes in the Allied command team. General Eisenhower had been sent to England to take command of the great force assembling there in preparation for the invasion of France. General Montgomery had also gone to England, to take command of the Twenty-First Army Group, under Eisenhower. The new commander of Allied Force Headquarters in the Mediterranean Theater was British Field Marshal Sir Henry Maitland Wilson. Lieutenant General Oliver Leese took over command of the British Eighth Army. General Alexander retained his position as commander of the Fifteenth Army Group, and General Clark continued to lead the American Fifth Army.

73

A heavy German infantry gun (lower left) mounted on caterpillar wheels, is prepared for attack against the Allies near ruined Carroceto, Italy.

The Anzio-Rapido Campaign

DURING the Winter Line Campaign, General Alexander's headquarters was working out plans for a different kind of attack. This attack was to begin late in January. While the Fifth and Eighth armies pretended to make a full-scale attack on the Winter Line, another Allied force would make an amphibious landing on the west coast of Italy at Anzio, more than 50 miles behind the German defenses, and near Rome. This force was the newly established VI Corps, made up of British and American units, and commanded by American Major General John P. Lucas.

General Alexander well remembered how close the Germans had come to driving Allied troops into the sea at Salerno. Therefore he wanted to be sure that nothing like that would happen to the troops at Anzio. Since he had only enough landing craft to land three divisions at one time, he knew that the VI Corps would be in serious danger if the Germans were able to concentrate several divisions quickly near Anzio.

Therefore he ordered both the Fifth Army and the Eighth Army to fight hard to keep the Germans so busy along the Winter Line that they could not send many reserves to oppose the VI Corps landing. The Fifth Army, in particular, was ordered to make as powerful an attack as possible across the Rapido River, just southwest of Cassino. The attack was to be made by American troops and a newly arrived French corps. After this battle had been going on for about five days, with German reserves drawn into the fight, then the VI Corps would make its surprise landing at Anzio.

The offensive began on January 17, 1944, with the Fifth Army

An American soldier walks past the rubble that was San Pietro, Italy, shortly after it was captured by the Allied Fifth Army.

British troops open the pre-bombardment attack of enemy positions in the Rapido River section of the Cassino front.

attack along the Rapido. German resistance seemed to be even more determined than usual, and the American troops had not yet recovered from their earlier exhausting and unsuccessful attacks against the Winter Line. Progress was slow. The Americans and French lost many men killed and wounded. It was clear that this assault, too, would be unsuccessful, but General Clark ordered the attacks to continue. The Germans must be heavily engaged when the VI Corps landed near Rome if the corps was to survive.

The VI Corps began its landings at Anzio just before dawn on January 22. Kesselring had learned something about the plan from his observation airplanes, which had spotted the transports and their naval escort at sea the day before. But the Allies pretended to be heading for northern Italy, and Kesselring was tricked into believing that the landing would take place north of Rome. The British and American troops of the VI Corps found little resistance to their excellently conducted landing, and were able to push inland quickly.

General Lucas now had to make a difficult decision. One possibility was to advance boldly to cut the Rome-Naples road, and possibly to seize Rome itself. In that case his three divisions, even if quickly reinforced, would be in danger of being smashed if Kesselring acted with his usual skill and vigor.

The other choice was to advance slowly, making sure that the beachhead area was secure, and that the units kept together so as to be able to support each other against the expected German counterattack. Lucas chose this course of action. General Clark, who was with him on the beach, approved. Military experts still argue about whether they were right or wrong.

One thing is sure. Kesselring *did* react quickly, efficiently, and strongly. By January 24 he had moved three divisions to the Anzio area, and they had established a thin line around the cautiously ad-

An American soldier runs for cover after an enemy shell bursts nearby on the beachhead near Anzio, Italy.

vancing Allied VI Corps. Additional German reinforcements rushed in from the Winter Line, and from France, Germany, and the Balkans. By January 28, all Allied forward movement was stopped.

Leaving the German Tenth Army, under General Vietinghoff, holding the Winter Line, Kesselring personally supervised the build-up of General von Mackensen's Fourteenth Army around the Anzio beachhead. On February 15, when bad weather made it impossible for Allied airplanes to take part in the battle, and difficult for gunners on Allied warships to fire accurately, Kesselring counterattacked at Anzio with about eight divisions.

The Allied front lines were pushed in considerably, and on February 17 one German spearhead almost broke through to the sea. The Allied defenders rallied, however, to stop the German advance, and then counterattacked on February 19. Bitter, violent fighting continued for several weeks, and German artillery ranged over the entire beachhead area. The Allies were unable to regain all the ground they had lost to the first German attack. But as they strengthened their defenses, and received more reinforcements, their foothold at Anzio was no longer in serious danger. By March, however, there was a complete stalemate on the Anzio front. The Allied troops had made a successful landing, but the Allied plan had failed completely.

Battle for Cassino

IN EARLY February, after the Americans had been repulsed at Cassino and along the Rapido, General Clark tried another French and American attack. This, too, was repulsed. Then the veteran New Zealand Corps, well rested, was put in the line opposite Cassino. They, too, were thrown back by the powerful German fortifications.

Behind the German lines, high on the mountain above Cassino,

Bombed-out Cassino, Italy.

was the ancient monastery of Monte Cassino. The historic old buildings were still occupied by Benedictine monks. During the many Allied attacks on the Winter Line near Cassino, the Allies had been careful not to let any of their artillery fire or bombs come near the monastery. The Allies were assured by the monks that the Germans had also respected the monastery, and that no German soldiers had come within its walls.

But now General Bernard Freyberg, commanding the New Zealand Corps, became convinced that the Germans had put observers inside the monastery, whose towers commanded a full view of the Allied lines. Freyberg believed that these supposed German observers could spot Allied concentrations, and were directing German artillery fire and counterattacks. When he was ordered to renew his attack on Cassino in mid-March, Freyberg refused to move until

Allied bombers had destroyed the monastery.

General Clark apparently did not believe that the Germans were using the monastery, and he tried to convince Freyberg that he could attack without destroying the monastery. Freyberg refused, and General Alexander then insisted that Clark destroy the monastery so that Freyberg would renew his attack.

On March 15 the monastery was smashed into rubble by a massive Allied air bombardment, and the New Zealanders immediately renewed their attack. But then the Germans did move troops into the monastery ruins, which now made an excellent fortification. These troops, combined with those holding the other positions of the Winter Line, soon stopped the Allied attacks again.

After the war it was proved conclusively that no German soldiers had made use of the monastery until after the Allied bombardment.

The Rome Campaign

DURING April and early May, General Alexander received many reinforcements from America and Britain. As these additional troops arrived, he reorganized his forces and prepared plans to renew his attacks as soon as the weather improved in May. To permit the Fifth Army to concentrate for an overwhelming drive along the coastal lowlands of western Italy, the left flank of the Eighth Army was shifted over to the west as far as Cassino.

Then, while the Fifth Army made the main effort near the coast, the Eighth Army was directed to keep the rest of the German reserves busy by another assault against Cassino. As soon as these attacks were well under way, the reinforced VI Corps, now commanded by Lieutenant General Lucian Truscott, would make an attack from the Anzio beachhead to cut the Rome-Naples road.

On May 11, the Fifth and Eighth armies began their attacks as planned. Once more the Germans repulsed Allied assaults in the Cassino area. Further left, however, French and American troops broke through the Gustav Line and began to threaten the flank of the main German position at Cassino. Kesselring was forced to order his troops to withdraw all along the line.

On May 23, Truscott's VI Corps — really a small army with seven divisions and supporting troops — began its attack from the Anzio beachhead. German defenses began to crumble. On May 25 the right flank units of the VI Corps had reached out to establish contact with the rapidly advancing left wing of the Fifth Army. The Anzio beachhead was no longer isolated.

Kesselring's withdrawal was hasty, but it was skillful. The Germans conducted a number of excellent delaying actions. Despite the rapid American advances, the Germans were able to get most of their troops back to a new line just south of Rome.

The British and American pursuit was too quick and well conducted to give Kesselring time to organize this new line for defense. He began to withdraw again. On June 4, Allied troops marched triumphantly into Rome. The pursuit was continued without pause. The Allies were finally brought to a halt on July 20 in front of a new German line along the Arno River, 160 miles north of Rome. Here Kesselring and his Germans dug in again.

An infantry patrol of the Allied Fifth Army advances cautiously across a bridge into German territory near Nettuno, Italy.

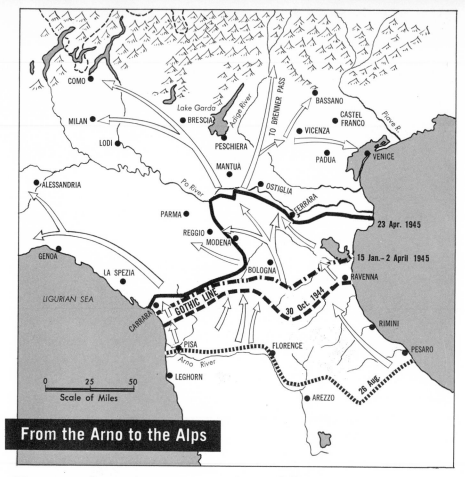

From the Arno to the Alps

From the Arno to the Alps

The Gothic Line

WHILE his advanced units held the Arno River in western Italy and the Metauro River in the east, Kesselring's remaining men constructed another deep belt of fortifications across the mountainous peninsula. This series of positions, called the "Gothic Line," was just as strong as the Winter Line, which had caused the Allies so much trouble during the preceding winter.

82

This time, however, the Allies were stronger than they had been when they first faced the Winter Line. Also, they had learned a number of lessons. During September and October, the Fifteenth Army Group advanced slowly but steadily through the German defenses until they got within 15 miles of Bologna, at the southern edge of the Po Valley.

Here they were faced by the strongest German defenses constructed in Italy. Here, too, the mountains were at their highest, and fighting became very difficult in the bitterly cold winter weather. Already exhausted by their desperate efforts of previous months, the Allies decided that they would not weaken themselves further with difficult attacks over rugged mountains in winter weather. Once more a stalemate spread over the Italian front.

Again there were some changes in the Allied command team. Alexander was promoted to field marshal, and replaced Wilson as a commander of the Mediterranean Theater. General Clark then became commander of the Fifteenth Army Group. Fighting General Truscott was promoted to be the Fifth Army commander, the British General R. L. McCreery replaced Leese as commander of the Eighth Army.

There had been a number of changes in the composition of the two Allied armies, also. Some additional veteran divisions had been sent to the Western Front in France, and these had been replaced by a variety of national units. The Fifteenth Army Group had always had many nationalities in its ranks. By the beginning of 1945 these units included: American, British, New Zealand, Canadian, Newfoundland, South African, Palestinian, Jewish, Brazilian, Gurkha, Indian, Polish, Italian and Japanese-American.

During this period Kesselring was called back to Germany to use his skill in bolstering the sagging German defenses on the Western

Front. He was replaced in Italy by General Vietinghoff. The Germans continued to improve and strengthen their defensive positions during the stalemate.

Allied Spring Offensive

FIELD MARSHAL Alexander and General Clark used the winter lull to rest their troops, to reorganize their armies, and to prepare plans for a powerful offensive in early April.

The final Allied assault began on April 2 with relatively minor attacks against both flanks of the German line. This was intended to make the German reserves spread out so that they would be unable to block the coming main attacks near the center of the line. One week later the Eighth Army began to smash its way through the left flank of the Gothic Line, in the lowlands southeast of Bologna. A powerful air bombardment assisted the British attack to break through the forward German positions.

On April 14, another overwhelming aerial bombardment signaled the beginning of the advance by General Truscott's Fifth Army. In four days of desperate fighting the Americans blasted their way through the last mountain range south and west of Bologna. By April 20, American tanks had broken through the German lines west of that city, and had begun racing through the flat, open country of the Po Valley.

Even though they must have realized that the defense was hopeless, the Germans had continued to fight with their usual skill and determination. But now, with both the Fifth and Eighth armies sending armored spearheads into the areas to his rear, Vietinghoff knew that his Gothic Line would have to be abandoned. Making a desperate effort, the Germans tried to break away from the pursuing Allies and to get back across the Po. But Allied aircraft bombed them incessantly, and Allied tanks slashed at the columns of German trucks and foot soldiers.

At the same time, many Italian civilians, who had received arms secretly from the Allies, now rose against the Germans. Roving behind the German lines in guerrilla bands, they blew up supplies and took a heavy toll of the retreating troops.

Although many of his men were captured by the Allies and by the Italian guerrillas, Vietinghoff did succeed in getting most of his troops back across the Po. But they had to abandon almost all of their heavy equipment, guns, and tanks.

Pursuing American units reached the Po on April 22, and began to cross the following day. By April 28, Allied spearheads had

German tanks and motor vehicles, destroyed by Allied air attack, form a jumbled mass of wreckage in a roadside ditch in Italy.

reached the foothills of the Alps, and General Vietinghoff knew that further resistance was hopeless. So, even though Hitler sent him radio messages insisting that he continue the fight, Vietinghoff secretly sent representatives to negotiate with the Allies for the surrender of the remnants of his armies.

One day earlier — April 27 — Mussolini had tried to escape from Italy with a German truck convoy. He had been captured and recognized by a band of Communist guerrillas, who brutally murdered him. This was probably a fitting end for the man who had himself been so brutal in leading his people into a terrible, bloody war which they had never wanted to fight.

On April 29, Vietinghoff agreed that his troops would surrender unconditionally four days later. Although Hitler was furious when he heard about this, he was himself near the end of his career. Berlin was surrounded by Russian armies.

The surrender in Italy was effective on May 2, 1945. American armored columns continued to race into the Alps and through the Brenner Pass, to meet other Americans advancing into Germany and Austria from the west. In less than a week, Hitler would be dead, and the war in Europe would be over. This great victory could not have been won so quickly without the hard-fought Allied successes in North Africa and Italy.

San Pietro, Italy. Bomb-wracked civilians emerge from the hillside caves to which they fled when the war came to their town.

Index